D1262421

Praise for *Foodaholic*

"As an addiction doctor I cannot think of a more serious addiction issue in our country than eating addictions. Ms. Keller's book is landmark for now and forever and will serve to help those without direction to find their way to a healthier lifestyle. I will recommend this book to all of my patients who can't seem to find a solution to their weight problems."
—David Kipper, M.D. Internist, Beverly Hills, Author of *The Addiction Solution* (Rodale)

"Irene Rubaum-Keller gains her knowledge both as a professional psychotherapist and as a person who has experienced firsthand the challenges of achieving and maintaining a healthy body weight in an unhealthy food environment. Her practical suggestions will help those struggling with these issues to find their way."
—David Heber, MD, PhD, FACP, FACN, Professor of Medicine and Director, Risk Factor Obesity Program and UCLA Center for Human Nutrition

"Irene Rubaum-Keller knows her stuff from the inside out. She's smart and down-to-earth in her approach and--most of all--she's living proof that her system works. Reading this book will be time well spent."
—Hope Edelman author of *Motherless Daughters* (Dell)

"Irene has lifted the fad diet into a zone of authentic healing. She brings expertise, wisdom, and lightheartedness into this must read book for those of us who thought we could live in denial...and munch chocolate in our closets. I'm Outed."
—Merrie Lynn Ross, filmmaker, comedienne, author of *Bounce Off The Walls- Land On Your Feet.*

Foodaholic

The Seven Stages
to Permanent Weight Loss

Foodaholic

The Seven Stages
to Permanent Weight Loss

Irene Rubaum-Keller, LMFT

MILL CITY PRESS

MINNEAPOLIS

Copyright © 2011 by Irene Rubaum-Keller, LMFT.

Mill City Press, Inc.

212 3rd Avenue North, Suite 290

Minneapolis, MN 55401

612.455.2294

www.millcitypublishing.com

All rights reserved. No part of this publication may be reproduced, stored in a retrieval system, or transmitted, in any form or by any means, electronic, mechanical, photocopying, recording, or otherwise, without the prior written permission of the author.

ISBN-13: 978-1-936780-75-4

LCCN: 2011932074

Cover Design by Sophie Chi

Typeset by Wendy Baker

Printed in the United States of America

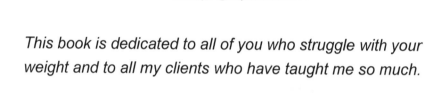

This book is dedicated to all of you who struggle with your weight and to all my clients who have taught me so much.

Contents

Introduction

YOU ARE ABOUT TO embark on a journey through the maze that is food addiction and weight loss. I will take you through the seven stages of getting honest and breaking free from your food addiction, eating issues and weight control problems. In this book I have identified the seven stages one must go through to lose weight, keep it off for good and overcome a food addiction.

Food addiction is real! Eating too much, too many calories, of highly palatable food is an addiction that affects so many of us. Of course we all need to eat to live, but food addiction is different. We can see the results when we look at the health of our country. 66% of Americans are currently overweight. Of that group half fall into the obese category. Obesity puts one at risk for heart disease, stroke, high blood pressure and certain cancers. It can be deadly and yet, we can't stop eating.

America's weight has been going up, steadily, since the 1970's. We have seen such a rise that we know it is not just a change in genetics causing this. Genes don't mutate that quickly. We believe it is caused by a combination of factors. For one, we are more sedentary than we used to be. Our food supply has changed as well. The introduction of high fructose corn syrup, highly processed foods that are cheap to produce and create cravings, are ubiquitous. The portion sizes have also increased and overall we are taking in more calories than we did in the 50's and 60's.

There is new and exciting research being conducted about food and its addictive nature. We have been able to produce sugar addiction in rats so strong that they go through withdrawal when the sugar is taken away. We also now know that the high fat, high salt and high sugar foods activate the same reward pathways in the brain as do drugs of abuse.

It is my mission, in writing this book, to help you break free from your food addiction, lose weight, get healthier, feel better and look better. I have done all of this myself! I lost fifty pounds, 20 years ago, and have kept it off since. I will share my story with you. I was a classic foodaholic.

I am also a licensed psychotherapist specializing in the treatment of compulsive overeating, weight management, bulimia and binge eating disorder. I have helped hundreds of people lose weight, conquer their food addictions, recover from bulimia and binge eating disorder. I'm writing this book to help you too.

To be successful you must understand the road to recovery both on the psychological level as well as the physical. To help you through it, I will take you through the seven stages of the journey, one stage at a time. Weight loss is only one stage on the road to permanent weight control and freedom from food addiction. The other six stages are just as important, if you want to be successful long term.

My interest in this subject began very early, as I was a chubby eleven year old. I went to my first Weight Watcher's meeting at the ripe old age of thirteen. Even though I was only slightly overweight then, it set me up for years and years of battling with my weight. It wasn't until I found the keys, which I will share with you, that I was finally able to lose fifty pounds and keep it off.

In my years as a professional therapist, I have met many amazing people, of all ages and from all walks of life, who have been successful at losing weight, keeping it off, and breaking free from their food addiction. I will be sharing some of their stories, some of my own, and incorporating the latest research findings in the field of obesity.

It is my hope that you will find your way to permanent weight loss and freedom from a very powerful addiction. If so many of us have been able to do it, you can too. We aren't super humans, we have just learned how. It is not easy, or simple, but entirely possible and worth the effort. There is nothing better than looking and feeling your best. No food tastes that good.

So come with me as we travel the sometimes bumpy road to permanent weight loss and freedom from food addiction.

1

Stage One
The Awakening (AKA OMG I'm Fat)

IT MIGHT HAVE BEEN a slow and gradual awakening or, as it was in my case, a sudden slap in the face. However this stage happened for you, it is the first step on the journey. That undeniable moment when you realize, Oh My God I'm Fat.

For some it might be a realization that you can't stop eating chocolate, or pizza, or Cheetos. You might try to avoid your favorite ice cream shop but are powerless to resist if you find yourself driving by. The car just pulls in all by itself. This awareness, that you are not in control, is the first step for some.

Most people realize they are fat, and/or have gained a lot of weight, before they admit they are powerless over certain foods. Whether you realize you have a food addiction, or you have a weight problem, the first step is to come to terms with the fact that there is, in fact, a problem.

My Story

It was after my break up with Mark, my gorgeous personal trainer from England (who looked like a cross between Tom Cruise and

Gilles Marini), that I became a food addict. I don't blame Mark (or Peter, or Fred, or Ed), or any of the guys who came before him, but as one addiction therapist likes to say, "Addicts trust substances, not people." Something in me just snapped after our break-up and I turned to food.

It wasn't like I woke up one morning and made the decision to be a foodaholic. Food had always been there for me in the past. Since I had been on and off diets since adolescence, I had a love/hate relationship with food. This time, though, it was all love. This was like a slow and steady slide into the nightly ritual that became my solace, my friend, my party and my lover.

I was just starting my career as a psychotherapist. I spent my days working out and then seeing clients. It wasn't a bad way to spend my time, and I actually enjoyed my work, and my work outs. I had no interest in dating though, as I had just been through a string of bad relationships, and much preferred to come home and just be alone after work. When I say alone, I mean without humans, but not without my food.

They knew me at See's candy. I'd go in and get the pound box and pretend it was a gift for someone. "Would you like me to wrap this?" "Yes, please!" I think they knew it was for me, but they played along.

There was my frozen yogurt run, my bran muffin phase, the pasta period and of course chocolate. I would come home from work and start eating until I passed out. Just like an alcoholic. I'd wake up with a food hangover, still full from the night's misadventures, and repentant. I would promise myself that I wouldn't do it again. I'd hit the gym, eat very little during the day and inevitably do it again the very next night. I was lonely, out of control and stuck. It was a helpless, hopeless and horrible way to feel.

I went to movies alone during this time with my muffins. I remember vividly watching a Kim Basinger film and feeling green with envy at her gorgeous body, all the while eating this huge muffin that had to be at least 1,000 calories. There were the many Saturday nights home alone with Famous Amos. Amos and I were very tight. One night, in particular, I was watching Saturday Night Live. Goldie Hawn was the guest star. I was feeling so envious of her cute little figure while devouring the bag of Famous Amos. I was thinking, "I'll never look like that." (Grab a cookie) "She is so adorable." (Another cookie).

I guess I knew I was gaining weight but my ability to deny that fact was pretty strong. I wore leggings, everyday, with big baggy sweaters and boots. It was quite stylish, at the time, and concealing (or so I thought). I avoided the scale, photos, clothes shopping and anything else that might have broken down my denial.

Then, one day, I was walking along in a store with mirrors on opposite walls. Some of the mirrors were at angles that allowed you to see yourself from the side. As I was walking through the hall of mirrors, I noticed a woman out of the corner of my eye. My first thought was, "Oh, she's a big lady." Then I got the courage to look a little more directly and noticed that the woman was wearing the same sweater as I was. As I was thinking about how funny that was, I looked closer and BAM!!!! I SAW MYSELF. Not the way I had been seeing me, somehow the denial carried over to my reflection in my usual mirrors, but in all my fat glory. That big lady was me.

That was my turning point. It was what I needed to get me to face reality and begin the process of doing something about it.

When you have battled with your weight, you may find it difficult to really know what you look like. It may be just as hard to see the weight gain, as it is to see the weight loss.

Fat Denial

Even though my confrontation with myself in the hall of mirrors was the moment I realized I was fat, when I looked back, I could see there were actually a lot of little moments that added up to that one, big, painful moment of clarity. There was the day I could no longer buy jeans at the department store. That was before Macy's had a large lady department. I tried on the largest size Macy's carried, which was a 14, and it was too tight. I asked the sales lady if they had size 16 (quietly as I was embarrassed that I needed that big a size). In what seemed like the loudest voice she could muster, almost like she pulled out a microphone for the entire store to hear she said, "I'm sorry, 14 is the largest size we carry. You will find what you are looking for at Lane Bryant." I had to lug myself to Lane Bryant to buy jeans. That moment didn't get me to the weight loss decision, as I was still in denial about the way I looked. The voice of denial spoke to me and said things like, "You may have some extra weight on you, but you are still beautiful."

There was the day in the movie theatre, when I couldn't put my purse down beside me on the seat. There wasn't enough room for my big body and my little purse. I had to hold my purse in my lap the entire movie. I guess at the time denial voice said, "Oh well, that's no big deal at all."

Since the weight gain is gradual, the changes are too. The

day I could no longer cross my legs was really a process of them crossing less and less as the weight came on. At my lowest weight, my legs could almost cross twice. You know how you can wrap the top leg around the bottom and hook your foot behind the top leg? As the weight gain was progressing, the hooking of the foot was gone, "Oh well." Then slowly my top leg began sticking out as my thighs were getting bigger. They would still cross but due to the size of my legs, the top leg wouldn't go down much and so my foot would stick out. I used to get hurt from people hitting that foot at they passed by. "Oh well." Then eventually, they just didn't cross at all. That's when denial voice said, "Leg crossing is for sissies." which is another version of, "Oh well." Denial is amazing.

There was the nurse at my doctor's office. She was a real gem. I told her I didn't want to know my weight, as my denial was in play, and asked her not to tell me. I didn't look when she weighed me and she didn't say anything. Then she took my blood pressure and I told her I did want to know what my blood pressure was. She said, "If I told you your weight, your blood pressure would go up." She was quite overweight herself, by the way.

You could be in fat denial if you are surprised when you catch a glimpse of yourself unexpectedly, or see a photo. When this happens, if you can't believe it is you because the reflection, or photo, is much bigger than you think you are, then denial is likely at play. Once you face your weight, you will most likely be willing to face the behavior that has caused the weight gain.

Study the Successful People

It is my belief that if you want to be successful at something, you should study the people who have done it before you. With weight loss, there really is no need to reinvent the wheel. We now have access to data on over 5,000 "weight loss masters" who can teach us how. The National Weight Control Registry began their study in 1994 and has been tracking successful losers since then. Their criteria for a "weight loss master" is a 30 lbs., (or greater) weight loss, and maintenance of that loss for one year or more. They have been releasing their findings as they come in and I will be sharing some of them with you.

77% of the weight loss masters began their weight loss journey due to a triggering event. Someone mentioned they looked chubby, or that they should skip dessert. They saw themselves in a store window, in a photograph, or like I did in unfamiliar mirrors. They went to buy their usual size clothing and found that they had to go up a size as nothing fit. They were told by their doctor that their weight was a health issue, etc...

For most people the triggering event was what broke down the fat denial. Breaking down that denial is necessary to progress to the next stage.

Triggering Events

Milly (all names have been changed) came to me to lose weight. She had gained weight while she was going through law school. She made the mistake of pairing studying with eating. She also found that she was using food to deal with the stress of school. Milly had always been thin, cute and sexy. By the time she got through law school she had gotten married and gained forty pounds. Her husband didn't mind the weight and she continued to gain for many years. Milly was in denial of how heavy she had become. She actually thought she was hiding her fat from everyone, and she was even hiding it from herself. She never got on the scale. She paid attention to her hair, make-up, nails, and accessories so she felt she always looked good. Then she and her husband took a trip. She got on the plane and went to fasten the seat belt and couldn't. Even with the belt fully extended, it wouldn't reach across Milly's belly. Suddenly, clearly and painfully, she realized she was fat. Really fat! She felt she had been hiding her fat from her husband, but since he was with her when she needed the seat belt extension, she realized the jig was up. That is what spurred Milly into weight loss mode. It was her triggering event.

Shelly is also one of my clients. She had always been heavy. Even at eight years old she was already on diets. She knew she was heavy but in some denial about how she really looked. Shelly is a nurse practioner and works for a gynecologist. She does the pap smears. One day a patient came in whom she didn't know. She said the woman weighed exactly what she weighed and was the same height. Shelly said this woman was so fat that she had to hold her thighs apart just so she could get the Pap smear. This was so gross to her that she was able to face her own weight for the first time. She realized the woman on the table was also her, and she didn't want to live that way anymore. That experience is what spurred Shelly into action. It was her triggering event.

Jim came to me to deal with his weight after he was jolted out of denial. He didn't realize he had gotten so heavy until he saw a photograph of himself. He saw his large, round face and big round belly and he couldn't believe it was him. He told me, "I can't understand how this could be? When I look down I see my legs and they look the same to me. Even when I look in the mirror I don't look as big as I do in this photo." I think he really wanted me to tell him that he wasn't that fat and that he didn't need to worry. That it was just a bad photo. Jim was still in some denial about his weight and not sure he was ready to give up the food. He was on the verge of being ready, but food was his greatest pleasure. He was wealthy and would have the best food in the world shipped to him. Lobster, caviar, cupcakes, steak, you name it! He knew not only the best places to have food shipped from but he also knew the best restaurants in town. I encouraged Jim to have more pictures taken in various clothes, sitting, standing, different lighting, etc… to get a more accurate picture. When he came to his next session he was horrified. He handed me a stack of pictures he had his friend take. For the first time, he was able to really see how big he had become. Those pictures were what triggered Jim into weight loss mode.

Karen, a good friend of mine, was out walking with her husband one day, when she caught a glimpse of a woman out of the corner of her eye. It was a reflection from a store window but she didn't realize that at first. Her immediate thought was, "That is an overweight, middle-aged woman." Then she saw her husband was walking next to this woman, and then, she realized that overweight, middle-aged woman was herself. Karen thought of herself as young, and hot, so how could that be her? For Karen, that was all it took to spur her into weight loss mode. At 34 she was not ready to be an overweight, middle-aged woman.

How Did I Let Myself Get Like This?

When I surveyed people and asked them when they first realized they were overweight, the majority said they knew it around puberty, ages twelve to fourteen specifically. Those people were teased at school and/or had relatives who would comment on their size. Being a chubby kid can be devastating. It is the time when we are just developing our sense of self and being heavy then can set one up for a lifetime of difficult psychological obstacles. Heavy kids often feel "less than", not as popular, etc... This age is critical in that there is a somewhat normal tendency for kids entering puberty to get a little chubby right before they sprout up in height. If too big a deal is made about their weight then, it can set them up with a fat self image that can be extremely difficult to overcome. Of course there are some kids who really are obese and do need to be more active and eat healthier food, but if you are the parent of a child, who is only slightly overweight, be careful. Encourage healthy eating and lots of physical activity, but don't label them fat or chubby so young.

25% of the people I surveyed said they were fat their whole life. From as young as three and upward, this group was teased, had critical parents and were put on diets very, very young. Many of these people said that when they look back at photos of themselves from that time period, they either weren't overweight at all, or only a little bit chubby. Since such a big deal was made of it at the time, it set them up for a lifetime of dealing with weight issues. Fat became part of their self-image, even if it wasn't appropriate. This is the group that has the highest tendency to experience yo-yo dieting into adulthood.

The other popular time the people I surveyed gained weight

was after getting married. This seems to be a time when there are big life changes and whatever routine had kept them thin, changed to one that added weight. Many were cooking more, snacking more and at home more than they had been before. There also tends to be some relaxation in that you are no longer looking for a mate, and if your mate gains weight with you then, why not?

Many women gained weight after having children. Of course it is normal to gain weight in pregnancy, but some of these women really let themselves go and had a very hard time getting their weight back down. This was particularly true in women who had more than one child and never got their weight back down between pregnancies. There was a tendency to keep adding more and more weight with each child.

Another common time people tended to gain weight was their first year in college. The famous "freshman fifteen", although the people I interviewed gained more like twenty five pounds during this time. It was the food, particularly dorm food, coupled with the stress of adjusting to college life that caused them to gain weight.

Law school seems to be extremely fattening. I have worked with many attorneys who put on a significant amount of weight in law school and have had a hard time getting it off. The extreme stress of studying hard, passing the bar, and even the first few years of being a new lawyer, have added up to lots of pounds for many people.

Regardless of the reason(s) for the weight gain, or the time at which it was gained, there has to be some awareness that one is overweight before one is motivated to do anything about it. Even with the understanding that one is, in fact, heavy, many people

I surveyed walked around that way for a period of time without doing anything about it. It is one of the most painful places to be.

So before you can even begin to lose weight, you have to admit that you need to. You have to get to that point where you can really see what you look like. You have to feel all the negative feelings associated with being heavy before you will go forward. You have to come out of fat denial.

You Can't Really See Yourself

The one thing on the planet you will never be able to see the way others do, is yourself. Unless you could take your eyeballs out of your head and turn them back at you, you are reliant on reflections, photos and what you can see when you look down. You cannot see your face.

There is both the physical reality of your inability to see yourself and the psychological aspect of self image. Our self image gets set somewhere along the way and regardless of the current reality, tends to have difficulty changing to reflect it. We decide very early what adjectives describe us: fat, thin, smart, handsome, cute, pretty, selfish... It works in both directions with weight. If you have always been heavy, and lose a lot of weight, you may not be able to see yourself as thinner. Conversely, if you had always been thin, you may not be able to see any weight gain.

Lorna had always been a skinny kid until she was 11. Even then, and into her mid-twenties, Lorna would have been considered thin. So when I first met her at the obesity clinic, where she was a patient and she weighed over 300 lbs., she told me she just recently realized she was fat. Lorna was 59 when I met her and had been very heavy for 35 years. She couldn't really see it but she could no longer walk without pain and her life was getting very small. She had enough awareness of her size to avoid having pictures taken. If a group photo was happening she would always hide in the back. Part of her had to know how heavy she was, but she just wasn't ready to do anything about it and therefore if she just ignored it, it was less painful psychologically that way.

Denial Comes in Different Packages

There are some tell-tale denial signals you may want to pay attention to if you are thinking that you might be a little overweight and/or have a problem controlling your food intake. As the weight goes up, there are the clothes that are too small. You can use denial here by picking only your larger and/or stretchy items. This will only last so long though, as you will outgrow these at some point. This type of denial also has a tendency to break down when you need to wear something unusual, like for a special event. You may need to buy something new if none of your old clothes fit, and the confrontation of picking that larger size can break down any denial you have. Sometimes, however, people will just decide that it's the clothing maker and their sizes are screwy.

When my Aunt Edie, who died of the complications of obesity at the age of 60, was gaining weight she found that she would hold a pillow over her stomach when she sat down. She thought the pillow would hide the fact that when she sat her stomach stuck out. When you are gaining weight you may think the pillow over the stomach helps, but it doesn't really.

Along with not being able to cross your legs, the heavier you get, you won't be able to tie your shoes or put on panty hose either. I was once fortunate enough to hear Etta James sing live in a small club. She was at one of her heaviest points then and had the audience on the floor laughing telling us the story of her trying to put on panty hose and how it was like a sling shot. She said she was lucky to have made it to the gig since the panty hose almost took her out. I have known people to wear only elastic waist pants and slip on shoes to avoid confronting their physical disability caused by their weight. A man I worked with hit his tipping point when he could no longer wipe his own behind due to his girth.

If you were a high heel wearer at your lower weight, you may notice that they are next to impossible to wear at a high weight. One of my clients said, "I can't wait to wear heels again. When I put them on now, I feel like a pig trying to do ballet." Oh well.

When I was thinner, I would cross my arms in front of my body. As I was gaining weight I slowly stopped doing this because my stomach was sticking out and my arms would rest on it. This would have broken down my denial if I paid attention to it. Instead, I just stopped crossing my arms in front of my body. That fixed that problem.

Summer used to scare me. The thought of putting on a bathing suit was terrifying when I was heavy. It's not such an exciting thought even being fit, but fat, forget about it. I would turn down invitations that required suit wearing and if I did go to the beach, or to a pool party, I would wear clothes. "Aren't you going to swim?" "Not today, I'm just getting over a cold." Liar, liar pants on fire. Oh well.

But I'm Not That Fat, Am I?

Even if you only have five pounds to lose, you are reading this book because you haven't yet learned how to lose it and keep it off. There is a tendency, in the early stages of weight work, to minimize the problem. Minimization is denial's good friend.

You might even think you are fine but your doctor, friend, spouse, cousin...told you, you should watch it. I have seen people with more than 100 pounds to lose who think they look fine and are only concerned because of their health. Denial can help you with this one. It likes to keep you stuck, don't forget. It doesn't want you to change, even though your current weight might be serious enough to cause you major health problems.

If you want to lose any amount of weight, this book will help you get there and stay there. It matters not whether the weight loss goal is 5 pounds or 205 pounds. The work you will need to do is the same. Of course it will take you longer to lose 205 pounds, than 5 pounds, but the process of losing and maintaining is exactly the same.

When Denial Breaks Down

After my confrontation with myself in the hall of mirrors, I went through the strangest process. At first there was disbelief. How could that be me? I'm young, I exercise, and I thought I looked hot, what happened? I didn't think of myself as fat, and no one ever mentioned that word to me. Sure I had to buy jeans at Lane Bryant but, well, …….

So I decided to try reality testing and ask a friend what she thought. I was fully expecting this particular friend to say something like, "You look good the way you are. You don't need to lose weight." When I did ask this friend if she thought I needed to lose weight she said, "Well, you could stand to lose a few pounds." I couldn't believe she said that. What? NOOOOOOOOOOOOOOOO………………………… It can't be true.

But it was true. I had the mirror, my friend, the nurse at the doctor's office, my legs weren't crossing, my high heels were put away and I had to buy jeans at Lane Bryant. No matter what I did from that moment on, the denial was broken down. I had to face the fact that I was fat. Denial was over and there was no turning back.

Once I decided to face it, I got on the scale. That was a tough move but a necessary one. I couldn't believe how much I weighed. I had been avoiding the scale, wearing stretchy clothes and denying the problem long enough to have put on about 50 pounds. Avoidance is fattening!

Face It to Change It

Paying attention to your weight is necessary to get it under control. You will be doing the opposite of what you had been doing to get heavy. If you got heavy by avoiding the scale, paying no attention to what you ate, avoiding mirrors, photographs, clothes shopping, etc… then you will need to do the opposite to turn it around.

So, before you can take the next step on your weight loss journey, you have to face yourself and your weight. This takes great courage. Imagine yourself as the powerful person you are and know that you can face yourself as you are today. You can come out of denial and accept the reality of your current weight. You can, even though it is painful, admit you are overweight and that you do, in fact, need to lose weight. You can get on the scale and look at the number. It's what you weigh whether you look at it or not, so I recommend facing it. You can slay the denial dragon.

It is easier to face the fact that you need to lose weight when you feel like you have the power to change it. Which, you do. Your weight is within your control. It may not feel that way, it may not be easy to get it under control, you may not be able to get down to a super skinny weight, but you can certainly lose weight and feel better. If Shelly, Milly, Lorna, Jim, Karen, myself and countless others have been able to lose weight and keep it off, you can too.

Chapter One Exercises:

1. Get on the scale. Don't be afraid, you weigh that number whether you care to look at it or not. Write that number down. It is your starting weight, not your forever weight. *Face it to change it.*

2. Have some photos taken. Front, back and side. Think of these as your before pictures you can show people when

you lose the weight. This is the best way to come out of denial.

3. Go try on some clothes and write down what size you wear. That is your before size. Imagine what you will do with all your big clothes when you lose the weight.

4. Cross your arms in front of your body and feel your belly. Try crossing your legs as well and note how far they cross, if they do.

5. Feel yourself. While standing touch your belly, waist, thighs and butt. Our sense of touch can be used to help motivate us. If we can't see it, we can feel it.

6. Give yourself some credit for being willing to take action. It takes courage to move forward, and the fact that you are reading this now means you have it. Take credit for each small success along the way.

2

Stage Two
The Decision

ONCE I FACED THE FACT that I was fat, I was motivated to change it. If you have been in some denial about your weight, once you face it, you will ultimately be happier. The reason is even though your denial was in play, it wasn't working completely. Living in denial only works some of the time and then, there is a part of us, that knows the truth. That part is like a buzzing fly that stops by and annoys us, goes away, but always comes back.

Fat Denial Takes Energy

In order to stay in fat denial, you have to expend energy. You have to avoid the scale, which is not generally an issue unless you go to the doctor and they need to weigh you. Since most of us do go to the doctor periodically, this confrontation with your weight requires denial work. I have had clients tell me that they don't go to the doctor specifically because they don't want to be weighed. This can be physically dangerous as some of these clients are skipping basic preventative health care. Clients have also mentioned doctor avoidance because they don't want to be told by the doctor that their weight is a health hazard. This reminds me of the little girl who will pull her dress up to cover her face thinking, "You can't see me now."

When you come out of denial and are willing to face your weight, you will be able to face the doctor again. This small change has saved lives. Julie, one of my clients, had a suspicious mole that she was not confronting in order to avoid the doctor. She knew it looked strange and was changing. She even did research on the internet and what she saw concerned her. Julie needed some help to face her weight. In my practice, I generally don't push people to confront their weight but Julie was at risk. I keep a scale in my office for people like Julie who need help with the emotional aftermath of weight confrontation. With me by her side, Julie got on the scale. She weighed 188 lbs. She was 5'4". Seeing that number was upsetting to her but also a relief. She knew she was close to that weight but didn't know for sure. She was upset with herself for having let herself get so heavy, but also grateful to me for pushing her to confront the truth. Once she was out of fat denial, she went to the doctor, only to find out the mole was skin cancer. Luckily for Julie it was still early enough to have it removed and the cancer had not spread.

Sometimes getting on the scale is the triggering moment when the decision is made to lose weight. For others, the number is so overwhelming they just feel like it's too much to ever lose and feel hopeless. The emotional fallout from the scale is part of the weight loss journey. Even if you have been getting on the scale all along, really facing the number takes courage.

I asked Cindy, one of my clients who had gained a lot of weight over a three year period, if she was aware she had been gaining. She said, "Well, not really. I just didn't do the math." I didn't understand. She explained that from 130 lbs. to 133 lbs. was only three pounds, and so that didn't really concern her. Then she stayed at 133 lbs. for awhile and slowly added two more. From 133 lbs., to 135 lbs. was only two pounds, and so on, and so on, until she reached 185 lbs. and saw photos of herself. Suddenly she realized that she was fat. Then she did the math and was horrified to confront the fact that she had gained 55 lbs. That was a big deal to Cindy. Beware of the creeping weight gain!

As I recounted in chapter 1, while I was practicing fat denial if I did have to be weighed, I would turn my back to the scale and ask them not to tell me what it said. This sort of worked but not really. Occasionally, whoever was weighing me would try and be complimentary by saying, "You carry it well." That one is along the same lines as, "You have such a pretty face." A complisult! What is really being said is, "You look pretty good for a fat person." And "You have such a pretty face, too bad you have to ruin it with that body." Lovely.

Fat denial requires you to avoid having photos taken, looking in the mirror, trying on clothes, wearing a bathing suit, running, hiking, biking, skiing, crossing your legs and/or crossing your arms in front of your body. This all takes work to keep it going.

Once you face the weight, you no longer have to work so hard at denying it. This will free up energy and allow you to be present with your current size. While facing it can be painful, you will ultimately be happier because you will be living more congruently and more truthfully.

Assuming you are willing to face it, then you have choices. You can choose to change it, or not, but at least you now admit there is a problem. All of the weight loss masters went through this phase. It's the movement from "I'm fat" to "Now What?".

OK I'm Fat, Now What

What happens after fat denial breaks down is generally a decision to change. The reason being, that walking around in a fat body is uncomfortable, unattractive and can be unhealthy. When you face it, all of the negatives seem to come into focus and often are the motivational tools needed to embark on the weight loss phase. Some people remain in the awakened phase for a period of time before doing anything about it, however.

The Most Painful Phase: Stuck

When I surveyed people and asked them if they stayed in the painful place of knowing they had to lose weight but weren't doing anything about it, 87% said yes. Only 13% realized they had a weight problem and jumped right into losing weight. There were many reasons for this.

For some, they just weren't motivated enough to do the work. There was a group of people who needed time to prepare for weight loss. They were mentally gearing up. Some were doing research to assess the best way to go about losing weight. Others felt hopeless and depressed for a period of time. This is the most painful phase of the weight loss process. Knowing you have to do something but not being ready, willing, and/or able.

Just as there are voices in your head that are denial talking, there are also voices that are trying to keep you from changing. Change can be scary. Even though you may be miserable at the weight you are currently at, you may not know what it will be like to be thinner and stay that way. The stuck voice says things to you like: "You fat slob. You will never change. You have tried all the diets and what happens? That's right, you never stick to them. You are hopeless. Besides, it's genetic anyway, so what's the point."

Have you heard this voice speak to you? It's not very nice. It tends to get really loud when you are in this phase of the journey. When you are aware you need to lose weight and are in the process of making the decision to do something about it. The more times you have been in this place, and perhaps even tried unsuccessfully to lose weight in the past, the stronger this voice becomes.

Your particular stuck voice will be unique to you and your experiences. It is not your friend but wants you to stay right where you are. In fact, it is very helpful to imagine what it says coming out of one of your friends to get a stark picture of what it is really all about.

Imagine your best friend saying some of the things stuck voice says. He/she calls and says, "Hey fatty! What's shakin? Oh that's right, it's you! Look, you have been fat for so long you're never going to change so why don't you just forget about it and have another doughnut. There is no hope for you."

Sometimes stuck voice will take a kinder tack. It might say, "You love your muffins. Why give up your muffins when you love them so much? You deserve to have things in your life that you love. Skinny people eat muffins all the time. What else will you have to give up? It can't be worth it!"

That's not a very good friend at all, if you ask me. A good friend would want the best for you and at a time like this might even give you a pep talk. That friend might say, "You will feel so much better when you drop the extra weight. You might even be able to include your favorite foods, in moderation, and still be thinner and healthier. You know you are looking at unhealthy foods as cherished love ones. They are actually poison. These unhealthy foods are making you fat, and if you don't change, might even end up making you sick. You can learn to live without some of them! I'm here to support you in the process." Now that is a good friend and a voice you want to cultivate within yourself.

Big Jim

Jim knew he was in trouble when his doctor told him that he was borderline hypertensive and type 2 diabetic. He told Jim that he needed to lose weight otherwise he would need insulin and high blood pressure medication. He also let him know that at his weight and height, he fell into the "morbidly obese" category. This also put Jim at risk for a heart attack and a stroke. Jim was only 35 but at 5'8" and 320 lbs., he looked and felt much older. It was getting hard for him to move around and he couldn't reach his feet to tie his shoes. He couldn't sleep well, as the weight was pushing down on his lungs, and it also made it difficult for him to turn over in bed. Suddenly, once the doctor said something, all these weight related disabilities became very clear to him. Like someone had poured cold water on him.

Jim had been in active fat denial for years. Since the weight doesn't come on overnight, he was slowly adjusting to being bigger. He just stopped crossing his legs, running, swimming and even clothes shopping. He would wear the same big pants and just change his top. He had 2 pairs of slip-on shoes that he would alternate, and that was the extent of his wardrobe. All shoes with laces had to be put away. He avoided having photos taken, mirrors, and even seeing people who only knew him when he was thinner. He refused to go back to his hometown, even though he desperately missed everyone there, because he was too embarrassed by his size to be seen. This might have continued had his doctor not confronted him and his health hadn't started slipping. Staying in this state of heightened awareness usually doesn't last long, as it is extremely painful. Knowing how fat he was, how unhealthy, and how limited he had become due to his weight, led Jim to the ultimate decision to come and see me for help to change.

But I've Tried So Many Diets Already

I know you have. I had too before I figured out how to do this once and for all. I can teach you how to lose it and maintain it without going on another diet for the rest of your life. In fact, 82% of the weight loss masters I studied had tried numerous diets, for years, prior to finally losing weight and keeping it off. This is actually normal.

Here is a partial list of the diets I tried before achieving permanent weight loss:

The Beverly Hills Diet

Weight Watchers

Optifast

Atkins

Fit For Life

The Diet Center

The Master Cleanse

There are many more but this gives you an idea of what I went through prior to achieving my goal. With the start of each diet there was the great hope that this was the answer. Of course, none of them work unless you stay on them for the rest of your life. I was not willing, or able, to do that and hence, I would gain all the weight back and more.

The pile up of diet failures made me feel completely hopeless. It made that stuck voice all the more powerful for me. It helps to know that most successful long term weight loss maintainers tried multiple diets before they achieved their goal. This does not make you a failure. You can do this once you understand the process.

I Don't Want to Give Up My Food

I know you don't. I didn't either. I was very attached to what I was eating when I was at my highest weight. I loved my big muffins, my ice cream, French fries and my evening binges that filled my nights.

I would bring one of my muffins to the movies with me and it made the movie that much more enjoyable. I LOVED my muffins. Of course I had to hold my purse on my lap with the muffin. Oh well.

My nightly stop after work at See's candy was the highlight of my day. I would look forward to that all day and plan out what I would get while I was at work.

Do not even think of getting between me and my frozen yogurt with fat free hot fudge sauce. It was what made life worth living. No matter that chocolate sauce is almost always fat free and that the fat free version has the same number of calories as the regular. That fat free label made it all the more fun!

The good news is if you follow my plan, you don't have to give anything up! You can learn how to include all of your favorites and still be thin and healthy. I know you don't believe me now, but you can! I still eat all those foods and have maintained my weight loss for over 20 years. It is completely possible. Stuck voice will tell you it isn't. It will say, "You will be like all those miserable skinny people who never eat a thing. What about your favorite sour cream, chocolate chip layer cake? You will have to give that up, you know." Stuck voice may even go on and list your favorite foods for you and tell you that you will have to say good-bye to them forever. Don't listen to it.

There are Only 2 Reasons to Lose Weight

100% of the people I surveyed, who lost weight, and kept it off long term, lost it for one of two reasons. Some had a combination of both, but it only came down to two things: Health and Vanity. That was it. People were either motivated to change because their health was at risk and/or because they hated the way they looked.

The older the person, the more health was the prevalent motivating factor. The younger people were more concerned with their looks. Generally younger people found they were socially hindered due to their weight. They were teased as kids, couldn't find dates as they got older and couldn't wear nice clothes. They felt physically inferior due to their size.

For others, they didn't want to die young. They wanted to be able to walk, run, play, dance and hike without huffing and puffing. They didn't want to have a stroke, or a heart attack, and they hated having to take medication for high blood pressure and diabetes. Their backs, knees, ankles and feet hurt all the time.

You cannot continue to eat exactly the same way you did and lose weight. That is the bottom line. Your weight is where it is today due to the choices you have made both in your food, your portions and in your activity levels. If you want to look and feel differently, you have to behave differently.

Fat is Beautiful

There is a movement out there called the Fat Acceptance movement. It was started in 1969 and is based on the sound principal that one should not be judged on outer appearance alone. They believe fat can be beautiful, just as thin can be, and that we need to raise awareness and tolerance for differences.

While I agree whole-heartedly that we, as a society, need to be more accepting of weight, age, sex, race, sexual preference, etc... I disagree with some of their justifications for being heavy. Many of them believe they are just genetically heavy and no matter what they do, they can't lose weight. Therefore, they should be accepted because it is their lot in life to be fat.

I believe fat is a choice. Anyone and everyone can lose weight if they take in less calories than they burn. Even if your genetics make it easy for you to be sloth-like and add fat to your frame, you are not a slave to your genes. This is also true if you have alcoholism and/or drug addiction in your family. You don't have to curl up on the couch with a bottle of vodka, or a vial of cocaine, and ask society to accept you as a drunk/drug addict because there is nothing you can do about it. Of course there is something you can do about it. Don't give in to the notion that you are powerless over your weight and can never be healthy and fit. The stuck voice would love you to believe that.

Is it harder for some of us to lose weight and keep it off? For sure it is. We are not all the same genetically, biologically or psychologically. Is it possible for all of us to be fit and healthy? I believe it is.

When our goal is health and feeling good, we can move in a positive direction. When the idea of vanity comes up in the obesity clinic where I work, our former nutritionist would say, "Use it as motivation. Whatever helps you get to your goal is a good thing." Some people make the decision to lose weight because they need to for their health. Others do it because they want to look better and fit into their clothes. Some want to not only look better but feel better as well. Whatever your reason for wanting to lose weight, in order to progress, you have to make the decision to do so.

I'll Do it Tomorrow

Many of us have made the decision to lose weight, or rather start a new diet, on Monday. This is the same strategy as waiting to take action until after the holidays, or after vacation, or after your birthday, etc…

Let's use the example of starting a new diet on Monday. Let's also say that you make this decision on Friday. What you are really saying to yourself is,

"I give myself permission to go crazy and eat everything and anything between now and Monday."

What this does is take the guilt out of overeating for a few days and allow you to really go wild. I used to do this when I hadn't yet learned how to control my weight properly. I actually used to think it was fun. I would go crazy getting all the foods I thought I wanted to eat and would get them in huge quantities. I would make plans to go out to eat at all my favorite places because, since I was starting this diet on Monday, I wouldn't be able to go back to those places for as long as I was able to stay on that diet. It was like the last supper that went on for three days. By the time Monday came, I was stuffed and ready to go on this diet. However, often by Wednesday, I would find a reason why I couldn't stay on this particular diet and end up blowing it. Meanwhile, I had over-eaten more calories in the three days leading up to the diet than I was able to deficit on the three days on the diet. This would end up meaning a weight gain for me.

The only way to lose weight is to make the decision to do it now. Start right now, no excuses. Did you already start thinking up some excuses as to why you can't start now? I bet you did. If so, once you read the action portion of this book and realize the only thing you have to commit to doing right now is keeping track of your calories, than there is really no reason not to start now. You don't need to go buy special food or a blender to mix up your diet shakes. You only need a pen and some paper. I would bet you already have that. Assuming you do, then you can start right now.

But I Don't Know How

You may feel like you have no idea what to do. I imagine you bought this book because you need help. The fact that you are reading this now means you are getting help. If you follow my plan, you will learn to get to your goal and stay there.

I know that stuck voice has something to say about that. It will say, "Ha, just another person trying to sell you their plan. Come on. You know none of them work."

What stuck voice doesn't know is that this is not a diet. This book will teach you how to be the weight you want to be and stay there permanently without once telling you what to eat.

Stuck voice would then say, "Oh yeah right. Like you can eat Snicker's bars and lose weight. This is hooey." No stuck voice, it's not hooey. A Snicker's bar has 280 calories. You can incorporate that into your daily calories and still lose weight.

Pain vs. Pleasure

It is a common belief in addiction medicine that the pain of the addiction has to outweigh the pleasure before one is willing to change. In the case of food and weight, the pain of being overweight, and all the negatives associated with it, has to outweigh the pleasure of the food before one is willing to change.

For Jim, even after his doctor let him know that he was a walking health risk, it still took several months before he embarked on the weight loss phase. He needed time to process the fact that he was fat. He was awake to the discomfort, the shame, and the limitations he now had due to his size. This hurt, both physically and emotionally. He had thoughts like, "How did I let myself get this big?" "What happened?" "I didn't think I was that fat or unhealthy."

After a few months of feeling sorry for himself, and eating even more than before, Jim made the decision to change. He was sick of being fat, tired, unhealthy and unattractive. He wanted to live a full life and at 320 lbs., that just wasn't possible.

Defeating the Stuck Voice

In order to defeat the stuck voice, you have to make the decision to change. If your decision is weak, stuck voice will keep on talking to you. It might go to sleep for awhile but when you waiver, it wakes up and starts spouting again. Be aware of this and you won't be thrown off by it if it happens down the road.

Stuck voice is a liar. It doesn't want you to succeed and even worse, it doesn't believe you can. Of course you can! If thousands of others have been able to lose large amounts of weight, and keep it off, than you can too. This is true no matter how many times you have tried and failed in the past.

Whether you make the decision fast, or slow, all the weight loss masters reached the point where they said, "ENOUGH". They hit that magic place where the pain outweighed the pleasure and they were off on the next phase of weight loss. They defeated the stuck voice and moved on to ACTION.

Chapter Two Exercises:

1. Make a long list of why you want to lose weight. Keep it handy and visible.

2. Be kind to yourself now. You may want to beat yourself up for gaining weight, but that can be fattening. Try and have compassion for your old self as you begin your weight loss journey.

3. KNOW that you can lose weight and keep it off. You don't have to keep living like this. Write a list of how your life will be and how you will feel when you are thinner.

4. Imagine carrying your sword with you and every time you hear stuck voice's lament, slay him. Remember, he's a diehard.

5. Focus on your health.

6. Decide to lose weight, now.

3

Stage Three
Action

THE FIRST TWO STAGES OF weight loss are complete and it's time to take action. You admit you need to lose weight and you have made the decision to do so. What's next? There are endless diets and diet programs to choose from. The number is astounding. If you feel like you need outside motivation, like you get from being weighed in and perhaps getting support from a group, you can find that at places like Weight Watchers, UCLA, etc... You can, however, do this yourself. This chapter will give you all the basics you need to get your weight under control.

First Understand Why You Are Overweight

When I ask people why they are overweight, most don't respond with the factual answer. The factual answer is that they take in enough calories, on a regular basis, to maintain that body weight. If you weigh 300 lbs. it is because you take in about 3,000 calories a day, if you are female, and about 3,600 calories a day if you are male. That is why you weigh 300 lbs.

When I ask people this question the first and most common answer is, "I don't know." That answer is followed closely in popularity by "It must be genetic. I don't eat that much and yet I weigh this much." I often notice a huge disconnect between the question, the factual answer, and the common responses.

I wonder still, even after 20 years in the field as an eating disorder therapist, how it is that people don't/won't take responsibility and acknowledge their part in their weight. An answer like, "I don't know." to the question, "Why are you overweight?" really means, "I'm not paying any attention to what I eat, how much, how many calories and/or if I exercise or not."

When I hear people tell me it's genetic, I hear, "I have given up trying." We know that genetics influence many things including our tendency toward alcoholism, addiction and how active we tend to be. You don't have to be a slave to genes. You can choose to fight against them and take control. You can make yourself exercise if your genetic tendency is toward sloth and you can refuse to drink if your genetics tell you that if you do you run the risk of being a raging alcoholic.

I also still marvel at the fact that people continue to want to debate the fact that "calories in/calories out" equals how much one weighs. I think this must be part of some mass denial. If I decide I'm fat because of some other reason, then I don't have to take control of my calories in/calories out (which by the way is the only way to lose weight). I can blame high fructose corn syrup, large portions served by most restaurants, my metabolism (which if yours runs on the slow side you can choose to eat less and/or move more, or be fat), my lack of ability to exercise, carbs, insulin resistance, hormones, etc...

If you feel like you are fat because there is something wrong with you physically, go get checked out by your physician. There are conditions such as: hypothyroidism, insulin resistance, hormonal imbalances, etc…that can effect the way your body processes the calories you take in. All the above conditions are treatable and none should be used as an excuse to stay fat.

So try separating your weight from your emotions for a moment. You weigh what you weigh because of how much you take in vs. how much you burn. How much you take in can be influenced by many factors, including emotions. People who have more awareness will tell me, "I gained 100 lbs. after my brother died and I used food to numb myself." Or "I gained weight after my wife left me." I call this grief eating. These people didn't gain weight because of their grief, they gained weight because they took in more calories than they were burning. They may have been doing so for emotional reasons but the bottom line is still calories in/calories out.

What's the Best Diet for You

The best diet for you is the one you make up for yourself, on a daily basis. Think about it rationally for a moment. Let's say I write a book that tells you exactly what to eat on a daily basis. I send this out to my agent, who changes some things, and then it goes to my editor at the publishing house. The editor changes things and gives me some notes too. Finally, we have a book that will be published. Eventually the book comes out and gets to you. This can take years. By the time you get the book you will be following a diet I made up 2 years ago while sitting in a Starbucks with my laptop. (By the way, most diet books were not written by nutrionists or registered dietians.)

I can guarantee you that when I was sitting at my computer making up what you should eat today, I didn't take some things into consideration. Things like: what you like to eat, what you ate yesterday, how you are feeling today, if you did or did not work out today, if you are going out to eat tonight and if so what type of restaurant, if you are full before you have finished the amount I suggested, if you are male or female, if you get migraines, if you are diabetic (or have any other health related dietary concerns), if you are perimenopausal, premenstrual, menopausal, young, old, if you would rather eat the dinner food for lunch and the lunch food for dinner, if you hate beets, etc... I made up some generally healthy diet that will create whatever effect I am claiming to give you in my book. This is not the best diet for you.

How To Lose Weight

All you need to know are some basic numbers and you can lose weight on your own. You need to know that to be the weight you want to be, you need to balance your energy in/energy out equation so it equals that weight. In other words, if you are female and want to weigh l30 lbs., you take that weight times 10 (times 12 for men) to give you your daily allotment of calories without exercise. Therefore, being female, if I want to weigh 130 lbs., I get 1,300 calories a day. If I burn an additional 300 calories working out, then I can eat 1,600 and still weigh 130 lbs. It is math.

Food has calories, which are units of energy that our bodies burn for fuel. Different foods have different amounts of calories with the lowest being fruits and vegetables and the highest being fats. If you eat low calorie foods, you can eat a lot.

It is good to eat small amounts often vs. eating larger meals spread out. This is due to the thermic effect of food. Each time you eat your metabolism goes up to burn the food. If you do this more often, you keep your metabolism going and you will burn more calories over the course of the day. You also avoid getting too hungry which is a set up to binge. We want to avoid this!

It is also good to eat some protein at each small meal as protein will keep you satisfied longer. A bit of good fat will as well. Think of the difference in how you feel if you eat a bowl of sugary cereal with nonfat milk vs. scrambled eggs. The eggs will take longer to be digested and leave your blood sugar steady. The cereal and milk are digested quickly and raise your blood sugar and then drop it again quickly.

Processed foods should be avoided at all costs. Your body is looking for nutrients and there aren't many vitamins, minerals, antioxidants, grams of fiber, or protein in a Twinkie. Our obesity epidemic has come on since the 1970's when high fructose corn syrup was introduced and portion sizes of cheap, processed foods grew exponentially.

Generally when I explain the math, people's eyes glaze over. Not because it is so complicated, but because it is both so simple and so hard. The simple truth is that if you take in more calories than you burn, you gain weight. If you take in less calories than you burn, you lose weight and if you take in the same amount of calories as you burn, you will maintain your weight. That's it. The glazing of the eyes, I think, has to do with what comes next. Once you accept that it is in fact calories in/calories out, then you have work to do.

Write It All Down

To be successful on your own diet you need to keep track of what you eat, how many calories, your current weight, and how much you burn in exercise. Not fun, I know, but if you are willing to do this you need never buy another diet book, join another weight loss program or listen to anyone tell you what to eat ever again. You can also eat whatever you want, within your calorie allotment, go out to eat, travel, never eat beets, eat your dinner food for lunch, etc... It completely frees you. It gives you full responsibility for your own diet and weight.

There have been times when I felt like I couldn't control how much I was eating. The only thing I could do was write it all down. This one step is crucial to losing weight and keeping weight off. The National Weight Control Registry has found that the most successful people at losing and keeping weight off, continue to monitor themselves on a daily basis, even just to maintain their weight. They either continue to weigh themselves every day and/or keep a food log. When you study the success stories, you learn how to do it.

One of the biggest studies ever done on the value of keeping a food journal was just published. In the study, of close to 1700 people, they found that those who kept a food journal lost twice as much weight as those who didn't. It is one of the most powerful weight loss tools we have.

Lucy was very reluctant to keep a food log. She came to me for therapy because she was sick of being heavy and yet didn't know what to do to change it. She was 24 and down to one stretchy black skirt that she wore daily. She refused to buy new clothes at her weight. She promised that as soon as she lost some, she would buy something new to wear.

Lucy finally began keeping records and slowly but surely, the weight started coming off. She learned about the calories in the foods she was eating and was shocked by some of them. She learned that her morning muffin had 800 calories. In order for her to weigh 125 lbs, her goal weight, Lucy needed to balance her calories around 1,250 per day. Her morning muffin meant she could only eat another 450 for the entire rest of the day. That woke her up and she quickly dropped the muffin breakfast. The day she walked into my office in black jeans was a very happy day. She has now reached her goal weight and maintains it by keeping records and exercising. She found 1,250 calories a day very hard to do, but with an additional 300 calories burned in exercise, she can eat 1,550 calories and maintain her weight.

Using Your Food Journal

Once you are keeping track of your calories in/calories out via a food journal, you can then begin to use it as a tool to help you change your habits. It is data that you can analyze and use to your advantage. For example, if you are having a problem keeping your calories down, you can begin to circle the foods you probably could do without.

When I was working my weight down, I found that between 9pm and 11pm I was taking in about 300 calories in fun food. I had already had dinner and even something sweet afterwards, but by 9pm I would feel like having something else. That was my old habit and I didn't FEEL like changing it. The problem was that I would have already had enough calories prior to the extra 300 and as a result, my weight was not where I wanted it to be. So for several days I circled the 300 calories on my records. Then I got the brilliant idea to still eat something at that time, but try and eat less calories. I was able to find a 150 calorie alternative fun food that I started eating at 9pm. Slowly the weight started to come down. I was still circling the 150 calories and then one day, I didn't eat them at all. The next day and for several days after that, I ate them again. Then I didn't eat them once again and gradually cut them out entirely. I could never have done that type of work without the food journal. I wouldn't have had that sophisticated data to play with and wouldn't know how to get my weight/calories under control.

The data in your journal will also help you understand why you overeat. You might notice that if you let yourself get too hungry, you end up having a high calorie day. Most "naturally thin" people make it a point not to skip meals. They know they need to fuel their bodies on a regular basis. This keeps overeating at bay.

You might also get clear on what foods you tend to overeat by paying attention. Are you having trouble stopping after two fun size Butterfinger bars? Does that have something to do with the fact that there is a big bag of them in the cupboard? If so, then you can take steps to reduce the amount of tempting, high calorie food you keep in the house.

The Scale

The scale is your friend. It is an informational tool that can help you get to where you want to go and let you know just how you are doing on your way to your goal. It is not the judge and jury. It is not the thing that determines if you have a good day, or not. It is just a tool and can give you data for your records.

Taking the emotion out of weighing yourself is important for the rest of your weight loss/maintenance journey. Without that tool, we wouldn't know where we were. It's like not asking for directions and spending hours and hours driving aimlessly around. The scale is like a compass that can tell you what direction you are going. It can also tell you how quickly you are getting to your goal and what is, and is not, working.

I have worked with hundreds of clients over the years who had scale phobia. Scale phobia and an irrational fear of confronting one's weight. The truth is you weigh whatever it is you weigh, whether you choose to confront it or not. By not looking at the number, it doesn't change your weight.

Practice using the scale as data only. Try taking the emotion out, both good and bad, and just use it as data. Of course you will be happy when you see the numbers going down, that's fine, but it's because of your behavior that the numbers are changing. Focus less on the scale and more on the behaviors you are working on making new habits.

How Often Should You Weigh Yourself

The best way to keep track of your weight is to weigh yourself once a day, write down the weight, and average it out over a week. Weigh yourself first thing in the morning and make that your routine. There is no need to get back on the scale throughout the day. Our daily weight fluctuations are not at all important in long term weight work. Pay attention to your average weekly weight and compare those weights as you go.

If you have ever been on a diet where you were weighed in once a week you know the pitfalls of that. There is the binge following the weigh in and then the desperate attempt to get it down by the next weigh in. You know how you show up in heavy clothing at the first weigh in, and by the end you are standing there, in front of people, in your underwear. You also run the risk that the day you pick to weigh is the day you put on 3 pounds of water weight. Daily weighing is best and the average will keep the water weight swings in perspective.

Snake Oil for Sale

In 1980, when I began to count calories and try to lose weight on my own, the labeling laws were not like they are today. Food companies didn't have to put the calorie information on their labels. There was one company that did, however, and I really appreciated that. They were so thoughtful that they said their muffin contained 140 calories, no sugar, no salt, nothing bad for you. I was thrilled. I figured I could live on 1,200 calories a day and could fit 2 of those muffins in at 280 calories.

Then, I began to gain weight. Here I was taking in 1,200 measly calories a day and exercising and I was gaining weight. How could that be? There must be something wrong with me, I thought.

So off I went in search of what could be wrong. I went first to my doctor who found that my thyroid was a bit low. This was great to find out and I thought was both the problem and the solution. He put me on a low dose of thyroid medication and I expected the weight to start falling off.

When it didn't I was really upset. In fact, it kept going up. I went back to the doctor and he rechecked the thyroid and with the small amount of supplement, it was back to normal. So that wasn't the problem.

I was seeing a psychologist at the time and he suggested I see another doctor. He sent me to the doctor to the stars. This doctor helped actresses and Playboy bunnies be slim. I figured this guy would be my ticket to Sveltesville. He examined me, weighed me and when I told him of my plight, and that I was living on 1,200 calories a day, and exercising, and yet I was gaining weight he said, "No one came out of the concentration camps fat." He then handed me a printed diet that he gave to all his patients and told me to follow it for 4 weeks and come back and see him then. No thanks Dr. Harsh.

Next, I decided to try the alternative route. I figured that Western medicine couldn't help me, so I turned to a naturopathic doctor. He told me, after doing muscle testing and checking my hair, that I had candida albicans and something else. The cure was to take all these supplements that he would sell me. This was expensive and didn't do anything.

What I finally found out, after years of trying different things, was that those lovely 140 calorie muffins actually had about 1,000 calories a piece. They were 10 oz. muffins, quite big, and the claim that they were only 140 calories was completely false. Since I was eating 2 a day, or 2,000 calories, that was why I was gaining weight. The company who made those muffins has long since gone out of business and since the labeling laws are stricter now, I hope this won't happen to anyone else.

When we realize calories in/calories out equals what we weigh, there is no room for snake oil. There is no need to take pills, colonics, try crazy temporary diets, eat only pineapple, don't eat after 6pm, etc... As long as you balance your calories, you can manage your weight.

As I write there are new calorie counting websites going up. Do a quick internet search and you will find excellent resources for counting calories and keeping track of what you eat. You can even keep your food records online and join multiple online weight loss support groups.

Sabotage

When Steve began to lose weight everyone around him was supportive. Steve was a behind the camera news man. He was about 150 lbs. overweight. Steve came to the obesity clinic where he did the liquid diet and lost all I50 lbs. He looked fantastic but he wasn't prepared for what happened among his coworkers. Women, who would never even talk to him before, were flirting with him. Although he liked that, he wasn't sure how to handle it. It was new for him. He even felt a little anger that these same women who barely spoke to him before were now flirting. He thought, "Wait a minute, I am the same person as I was, just smaller, and now I am worth talking to?" He wasn't prepared for that.

With the weight loss, Steve's look changed dramatically and he was asked to go on camera. This really sent some of his coworkers into a tizzy. They all really liked Steve but some of them were now profoundly jealous. As a result, he noticed that they were trying to tempt him with his favorite high calorie foods. He didn't give in but had to work through the unexpected feelings of those around him.

When we change, everyone around us has to change too, to accommodate the new us. Even though the people in our lives love us, and want us to be healthy and happy, they don't want to have to change themselves. In other words, they don't like it that they can no longer go to the fast food restaurant with Steve because he doesn't eat like that anymore. They might try to get him to go back so they feel more comfortable. They may not like it that Steve is now getting all this attention. They may try to take it away from him in some way. This isn't evil, or mean, it is actually fairly normal.

Steve's story is a version of sabotage that comes from without. Megan had her own version of sabotage.

Megan had been 300 pounds when she decided to take action and lose weight. She was very successful and was able to lose 160 pounds. At 140 pounds Megan was attractive and felt much better about herself. Big Megan used to stay late at work. She didn't date or have many friends, so her coworkers would ask her to do their leftover tasks for the day. Megan suffered from extremely low self-esteem and let people take advantage of her. When she got thinner, she decided to go work out after work and began to say no to her coworkers. They didn't like this, of course, and wished Megan would return to her former self. They would bring tempting food and have it near her, trying to entice her back to her old ways. This wasn't because they were mean, bad, awful people, they just liked the old Megan and the fact that she would help them out. They wanted her back.

Megan was smart and got into therapy to work on her low self-esteem. She learned to say no and feel OK about it. No was not in her vocabulary before and it was hurting her. She would do things for others and then resent it, but felt like she didn't deserve better. She was such a people pleaser that she wasn't even on her list of priorities. Everyone else was, but not Megan.

She was able to keep her weight off and eventually the people around her adjusted. It took a long time though. There were a few people who Megan had to say good-bye to. She realized that the few people she thought were friends were really just using her and didn't want to adjust to her new way of being. There was an empty period between when she let go of her old self (and related people) and formed new friendships. This is a weight loss hurdle all its own.

It is during this time that the sabotage voice starts chatting wildly. It says things like, "See, all this hard work and look what happens. You lose your friends and no one likes you. What's the point? You're thinner but still alone and miserable." Nasty voice!

Filling the Emptiness AKA Emotional Eating

When Megan felt empty in the past, she would eat. When she felt lonely, she would eat. She realized that she was using food to fill up her life and that it was unhealthy. The problem was she didn't know what else to do.

Just like with any substance that one can abuse, you have to be willing to feel a certain amount of discomfort when you give up that substance. The willingness to feel your feelings, instead of eat them, is very important.

Megan had to be willing to just feel empty and lonely. The awareness of these feelings propelled her to fill up her life in healthier ways. She started going to a gym where she began to make new friends. She also joined a weight loss support group and met new people that way. She took up knitting so she had a new, fun thing to do when she was home. She also found it kept her hands busy when she was watching TV, which was a high eating time for her.

Now when Megan feels empty or lonely, she either calls a friend, or gets out of the house. If she leaves the house she might go to the gym, take a walk, or go to a local Starbucks where she gets a coffee and just hangs out around people. She has learned to fill up her life with new people and enjoyable activities.

From Megan's example, you can see that changing your weight and eating habits, often means an entire life change. Megan's old life was one of loneliness and long work hours. Her new life is balanced with work, friends and hobbies. Food is no longer the central focus and sole pleasure for her.

In order to change your emotional eating patterns, you have to be aware of them. You have to acknowledge that you are using food to soothe yourself and eating when you are not hungry. You have to be aware if when you reach for food if it is because your body needs nutrition right now, or you need something emotional. You also have to be aware if you are eating past the point of full to anesthetize yourself. If you eat enough, think really full after Thanksgiving dinner, you get a little high. The high is a bit like a downer drug would give you. You get that relaxed and sleepy feeling. Some of us overeat on purpose to produce this relaxed, sleepy state. We can become addicted to this feeling if we produce it often. It is a way of tuning out and numbing out, just like taking codeine, vicodan, or oxycontin. Eating and food are very much like a drug when used in this way.

Once you become aware that you are using food as a drug, you can make changes. You can begin to ask the question before you eat anything, "Am I hungry?" If the answer is no, you can then begin the task of asking yourself and identifying, "What is it I really need and/or want?" If you are not physically hungry, what you need and want cannot be found in the refrigerator.

Sabotaging Yourself

It is one type of sabotage to work through when people outside of yourself are less than supportive, it is quite another when it is coming from within. When you are fighting with yourself to get to your goal and getting in your own way, it can be a tough fight.

Just as the people around you are uncomfortable with change, you may be as well. This might be true even if the changes are what you think you want, like weight loss. You may think you are ready, willing and able to lose weight only to find yourself blowing it after a short time on the weight loss path.

Bill thought he wanted to lose weight, as his weight was causing him physical discomfort and he hated the way he looked. He would make short attempts to control his calories and lose a couple pounds and then go right back to his usual eating habits and gain the few pounds back. He couldn't understand what his problem was. Bill's weight was up to 350 pounds and was physically painful for him.

Bill came to therapy to deal with the underlying causes of his weight issues and found that his weight had much more to do with deeper issues than just the fact that he liked food. If you try to lose weight and keep stopping, psychotherapy is a good option. It is difficult to work on issues you don't even know you have. Bill had been using food, and his weight, as coping skills for so long he no longer understood why. He just knew something was keeping him from being a successful loser.

What he discovered in therapy was that he was using both food, and his weight, to keep people away. He had been very hurt in relationships, throughout his life, and felt safer being big. Not only did he feel physically and emotionally safer being big but he got a lot of pleasure from the food. Since he didn't have much else in his life that brought him pleasure, it was very hard for him to give up the food and just deal with his life the way it was. If you recognize yourself in Bill, in that you start out fine, lose some weight but then stop, you may need psychotherapy to deal with your underlying fears.

I also recommend adding in some alternate pleasurable activities, even before you start to lose weight. Bill took up swimming and chess. He also got a jigsaw puzzle going at home to keep his hands and brain occupied. These lifestyle changes, in combination with working through some of his old feelings of hurt and learning new coping skills in therapy, allowed Bill to move into the action phase and stay there. As of this writing Bill has maintained a weight of 180 lbs. for two years now. He feels 100% better in everyway and has even started dating. His only regret is that he spent so much of his life in a big, unhealthy body.

When you look at all the things that change when you embark on the weight loss action phase, this self sabotage makes some sense. First of all, your eating habits will be different. What we eat is part of what makes us feel comfortable, normal, like ourselves, etc... We all have routines and habits that carry us through our days.

You wake up, get out of bed and head to the bathroom. Habit. You take a shower or bath in the same way each time. You drive to work the same way. Habits... routines... we need them. If we had to think about all the mundane tasks we do everyday, we'd have no room to focus on anything else. When you get up and head to the bathroom, if that is your routine, you are probably thinking about things other than getting up and heading to the bathroom. You might be thinking about your dreams from last night, what you are going to do today, etc... not teeth brushing, peeing and whatever else you do every morning in the bathroom.

The same is true of our eating habits. You most likely eat either the same things, or similar things, every day. If what you eat and drink is keeping you fit and healthy then your eating habits are working for you. If, on the other hand, your eating habits are causing you unwanted extra weight, then they aren't working and should be changed.

How do you change a bad habit?

First you have to be aware of it.

Some of our habits sink below the conscious level and operate without us even thinking about them. If you want to change your eating habits, or some of them, write down everything you eat and drink (if it has calories). Get your eating habits out of your head, and down on paper so you can look at them. Write down how much you are eating and the calories in the foods you eat. You might have to weigh and measure your food to learn the portion sizes at first. You can look up the calories online and there are numerous apps and websites that allow you to keep your food records online for free. You don't need a degree in nutrition to learn this information, however, you do need to pay attention and realize that what you put into your body is important.

It is estimated that we make about 200 decisions a day when it comes to what and how much we consume. Many of those decisions are unconscious, or habits. When your habits are working for you and contributing to your health and well being, life is sweet. When your habits are self destructive, well, the consequences are there and although habits can be very hard to change, they can be changed.

So part of your self-sabotage may just be your way of trying to feel comfortable by returning to your old eating habits. The awareness of this can sometimes be enough to nip it in the bud.

The Shock of Looking Different

Another aspect of self sabotage can come from being uncomfortable with your new size/body. Just as Steve was dealing with the changes in the way those around him treated him, Emily was running in the other direction. After losing 50 pounds Emily was unprepared for the attention she was getting from men. Being heavy, especially in Los Angeles, Emily felt invisible. She got very little attention from men and women were friendly to her. When she lost weight suddenly men were attracted to her and began to talk to her and even ask her out. Even though Emily really liked the attention, and wanted to date, it scared her. She had not had great experiences with dating and was terrified to try it again. Part of her weight gain had been an attempt to avoid that entire aspect of life. She was lonely, and sick of it, but the dating idea caused her to want to go back to her old ways.

Emily was also unprepared to handle the way women treated her now. When she was heavy, women were friendly or neutral. When she got thinner she noticed women glaring at her and looking at her up and down. She realized it was just jealousy but it threw her off. She wanted to say, "Hey, women, I am the same person you were nice to 50 pounds ago."

Through therapy, Emily was able to work through these fears and keep the weight off. She learned to navigate life as a thinner person. This is necessary in order to keep the weight off. Over time, Emily began to date and met a really nice guy. They are still together as I write and last I heard were planning to get married. She also learned to deal with the negativity from other women. After keeping her weight off for 3 years, she told me that she doesn't even notice that anymore.

Bill had also realized, through therapy, that he was using his weight as protection. We think of this mostly in women, but men experience it too. At a high weight Bill didn't have to think about dating, which scared him, and he felt safe being big in that he thought no one would mess with him. Once Bill was aware of these things, he was able to work on them and ultimately lose weight.

Exercise

Exercise is a good thing. I don't think you need me to tell you that. Since our weight is determined by calories in vs. calories out, it makes sense to up the calories out if we can. Most of us can do some form of exercise even at a high weight. The best exercise for you is one you enjoy and one you will actually do.

Lorna was at such a high weight that most forms of exercise were impossible. It was hard for her to even get in and out of a chair. She weighed 265 lbs. and even walking was difficult. The one exercise Lorna could do was water aerobics. When you are in the water you are buoyant and can move easier. She joined her local YMCA and started going to the water aerobics classes there. She loved them and her weight began to come down. As it did she was able to walk and added that into her exercise routine. She could only walk a block at first but now, as her weight has decreased, she can walk a mile.

Once Milly faced her weight the reality of how it felt to carry that much extra poundage hit her hard. She was motivated to lose weight after needing to get the seat belt extension on the plane and she could no longer deny the fact that it was hard to even walk around. At 225 lbs. and 5'2" she was carrying a lot of weight and needed a cane to walk. Her feet, knees and hips hurt all the time. When her husband wanted to take a trip to Europe, she realized that she wouldn't be able to enjoy it because she wouldn't be able to get around. That was the last straw for Milly and she began the weight loss action phase. She found a gym that was perfect for her and started going several times a week. After losing 75 lbs., Milly's husband took them on a long European vacation where she was walking, climbing and enjoying a great trip.

You don't have to exercise to lose weight. You can simply cut the calories in part of the equation but I don't recommend that. As soon as possible, you should start moving more. It's good for your heart, lungs, muscles, joints and moods. Most of the weight loss masters, those who have kept 30 or more pounds off for a year or more, exercise. As your weight comes down, you will most likely feel like moving more.

A recent study has come out that suggests that how much we tend to move, or feel like moving, may be genetic. You may have sloth in your genes. People who fidget burn more calories every day than people who don't. Our fidgeting factor appears to be genetic. While that is interesting, it doesn't really help us in our battle against weight. It lets you know that if you are a sloth, it may be harder for you to get yourself to exercise, but it is not impossible. You don't have to be a slave to your genes.

Keeping Things in Perspective

One of the most important things to keep in mind now is that this weight loss phase is merely one step in the weight loss journey. It is not the ultimate step, the only step, or even the most important step. Rachel lost 100 lbs. with counting calories and exercising. She said she had to decide that she was now a person who exercises and eats healthy. She didn't think of herself as someone who was on a diet trying to lose weight. She has kept the weight off for 10 years and she says it gets easier with time. She still exercises, counts calories and weighs herself everyday so she doesn't go back to her old habits. Sometimes, when life really gets her down she does go back to her old habits and gains some weight but she catches it before it goes very far and gets right back on the horse.

While losing weight is important, and why you bought this book, you need to understand that what follows is just as important as what came before. In order to keep the weight off, your work needs to continue.

Chapter 3 Exercises:

1. Begin keeping a food log and write everything down that you put into your body that has calories. Learn the calories in the foods you eat and practice learning about portion sizes. Weigh and measure your food for long enough to get good at estimating the portion size. You will be surprised at what a cup of pasta looks like on the plate. It's not very much.

2. Figure out what you would need to do to be the weight you want to be. For example, if I want to weigh 130 lbs. I need to take in 1,300 calories a day, without exercise. Attempt to do that. If you can, all you need to do is continue that once you reach your goal and you will stay there. If not, do the best you can.

3. Enjoy the process of losing weight. There are few things you can do that feel as good and look as good.

4

Stage Four
The Plateau

MOST DIET BOOKS BEGIN AND end with the diet, which is only the third stage in the weight loss journey. I believe this lack of understanding of the process is partly why people have such a hard time losing weight and keeping it off. For most people it is all about the diet. I am writing this book because unless that changes, we will still be a heavy nation.

During the weight loss phase there will be obstacles to tackle. If you know the quest stories in mythology (think Holy Grail), the story usually begins with a journey to get something or accomplish something. Along the way there are obstacles that one must successfully get past in order to get the Grail. It is the same with weight loss.

As you lose weight there may be a point when the weight loss begins to slow, or temporarily stop. People get off the train here. Successful dieters keep going and work through it. The plateau challenges one's motivation when the rewards stop coming as quickly or easily.

At the obesity clinic at UCLA, where I work, many of the patients are on a liquid diet. Even taking in as few as 800 calories a day some will not lose anything for a week or two and then suddenly drop 2 or 3 pounds the third week. Some patients leave the program after two weeks of no weight loss. They give up. If you want to be a successful loser, giving up is not an option. You must slay the plateau dragon to get the Holy Grail.

Why Weight Loss Slows Down

If you recall from the action chapter of the book, in order to determine the amount of calories you need per day, you take your weight and for women multiply it by ten, for men use twelve. As you lose weight, that number will go down. For example, if I used to weigh 200 lbs. then it took 2,000 calories a day to maintain that weight. If I drop down to 180 lbs. then it only takes 1,800 calories per day to maintain my weight. The less I weigh, the less I burn just to maintain my body.

This slow down comes about because let's say you are taking in 1,500 calories a day. When you weigh 200 lbs. you are deficiting 500 calories a day, which will produce a weight loss of one pound per week. When you weigh 180 lbs. and are taking in the same 1,500 calories, you are now only deficiting 300 calories a day. Since you must deficit 3,500 calories to lose a pound of fat, you can see how this will now take you longer. At 180 lbs. it will take you about 12 days to lose a pound if you continue to take in 1,500 calories per day.

Weight loss can also slow down if you drop your calories too much and the body thinks it's starving. Since our biology is still programmed for caveman days, we have a built in mechanism to preserve ourselves in case of starvation. The body will lower its metabolism in response to severe calorie restriction. This is why it is best to proceed slowly so the body keeps burning calories at its normal rate.

In addition to metabolism slowing if you cut down too much, you can also lose muscle mass. Muscle tissue burns more calories at rest, than fat tissue does. This is why men get to take in more calories than women. They have more muscle mass and therefore burn more calories at rest than we do. Lucky men. The key here is not to cut your calories too drastically, so that the weight loss is slow and mostly fat loss. In addition, it is very helpful to add in some weight training exercise to not only preserve the muscle mass, but to tone and add muscle so that you can burn more calories at rest. Since we tend to lose muscle as we age, this is an excellent anti-aging strategy as well.

Your Body is Not a Machine

Sometimes weight loss can slow for no apparent reason. This is one of the most frustrating aspects of doing this work and one of the most difficult, psychologically, to overcome.

Lucy was keeping diligent records, losing about a half pound a week, and feeling good about herself, for the first time in a long time. Then, for no apparent reason, even though her food records said she should have lost a half a pound, her weight stayed the same. That first week she was able to take it in stride and she just kept plugging away. When she came in the next week, her food records said she should have lost another half pound and yet her weight was up a pound.

"This is bullshit," she said as she threw the records down on the chair. Lucy was really angry.

"You must be really upset, I know how hard you are working, but this happens sometimes," I tried to reassure her.

"This is BULLSHIT. I have been working my butt off and I don't deserve to be up a pound. I should be down at least another pound by now," she screamed.

It took me awhile to talk Lucy down from her anger, but once she calmed down, she was able to accept the fact that her body was not a machine and wouldn't perform exactly as she wanted it to week after week. She also had to learn that in order to gain a pound of fat, she would have needed to overeat 3,500 calories above her maintenance calories. She knew that wasn't the case and so she had to believe me that what was happening was a water weight swing.

When you are losing weight, the body will sometimes hold onto water, for no apparent reason. Sometimes this water can stick around for awhile and make the weight loss appear to stop or even reverse itself by a few pounds. This needs to be understood as you progress or you might just give up and let the plateau dragon slay you. Don't!!!

Lucy was able to keep plugging away and then, about 2 weeks later, dropped 2 pounds instead of the 1.5 she had predicted she should have lost. Sometimes hormones, sodium, carbohydrates, a change in bowel habits, or just plain mystery can cause a water weight gain.

Muscle Weighs More Than Fat

If you are working out more than you did and gaining some muscle, the scale might not move as much, or as quickly, as your records might predict. This is so because muscle tissue weighs more than fat. The more muscle tissue you have, the more you will weigh. This is why men tend to weigh more than women; they have more muscle tissue than we do.

Muscle tissue is also denser than fat tissue so although the scale might not be moving super fast, you will still be losing inches. Fat tissue sort of spreads out where as muscle doesn't. You will also be stronger and feel more toned.

The best part about adding muscle is that it burns more calories at rest than fat does. Fats main purpose in the body is to be there as stored energy if you ever need it. It also cushions the organs, affects our hormones and insulates us from the cold. It doesn't require much blood, or energy to keep it alive.

Muscle tissue, in contrast, is dense active tissue that requires blood and calories to keep it functioning properly. It is metabolically active tissue.

So, don't be afraid to work out and add muscle. It is the best way to stay fit, toned and young. Just be aware that it might cause a plateau here and there. It's worth it!

How to Get Past the Plateau

The only way I know to get past a weight loss plateau is to just keep going. There is a saying in the twelve step programs that is, "Do the work and stay out of the results." That one is extremely hard to accomplish but is worth shooting for, especially when the work seems to be having less of a payoff than it used to.

Michael was at a plateau for two years. He was one of the clients I worked with at the obesity clinic. He lost 100 lbs. and got stuck there. Even though he still had about 50 lbs. to lose, he was stuck at 250 lbs. Michael was frustrated that he wasn't dropping more weight. In fact, he was so frustrated that he started eating more, his old coping skill for dealing with frustration, and in fact began to gain weight. This really upset him but since giving up was not an option Michael chose to work through it. He started keeping careful food records and was able to stop his weight from going up further.

Getting stuck at a weight on your way down to your goal is actually normal, and in some cases even a good thing. Most people who have dieted for years aren't very good at, or used to, maintaining weight. They tend to be good at losing and gaining but maintenance is a whole other animal. Maintenance, at a weight that is higher than you want to be at, can be uncomfortable but it is actually an important part of learning to keep the weight off.

For Michael, he was stuck at 250 lbs. because he needed to hang out there for awhile and get the hang of maintaining 250. He was used to maintaining 350 lbs. so 250 lbs. was not normal for him. It was work for him even just to stay there. He wasn't expecting this. He thought he would get straight down to the weight he wanted to be at, and then stay there effortlessly. He expected the journey to the weight to be difficult, but he wasn't prepared for how hard it was to maintain.

At 250 lbs. Michael was able to eat 3,000 calories a day, without exercise, to maintain his weight. The trouble was Michael was used to eating 4,200 calories a day, which is what he ate to maintain 350 lbs. That is a 1,200 calorie a day difference and to Michael, was a lot. So I encouraged Michael to just stay at 250 lbs. and learn to get comfortable there. This took two years. Michael is in his 60's and has had a weight problem most of his life. When most people hear how long this process can take, they want to run back. This is one of the weight loss dragons. We need to learn to slow down and allow time for change. When you think of how many years Michael overate, and was heavy, it is unrealistic to think he would just lose it and maintain the loss in a short period of time. This process should take years if it took years for you to build your bad habits.

In doing the research for this book, I found that 85% of the people I surveyed, who were successful at losing weight, and keeping it off, hit plateaus along the way. That is a very large number. Of that 85%, all of them said they just kept going. They didn't allow plateau dragon to take them down.

Allowing Time for Change

I was once at a cafeteria that was about two blocks from the beach. I was standing in line next to these two young women who were chatting as they were picking out their food. One said, "Is there any way to lose 14 pounds between here and when we get to the beach?"

That feeling of just wanting the weight off is normal. The idea that you can lose 10 pounds in two days is drilled into us by these bogus weight loss infomercials, lame diet ads and people willing to lie to sell you a quick fix that doesn't work.

In fact, just last night, my husband and I were at the bookstore checking out the magazines. I went to the fitness/women's/ health section and wrote down some to the lead articles. Here is a sample:

"Get a Firm Body in One Week Without Exercise"

"Lose 6 Pounds in 7 Days"

"Fast Food That Won't Make You Fat"

"Drop a Size Without Dieting"

"Bikini Body Now"

"Get Fit Fast"

"How I Lost 10 Pounds Fast"

What do these titles tell you? They tell me that we want easy and quick ways to achieve something that isn't going to be easy or quick. It also tells me that these types of articles sell magazines. The more magazines they sell, because you bought it with the hope of losing 10 pounds just by reading that article, the more articles we are going to see just like these. The more we believe these articles, the more frustrated we are going to get with the truth of how long and slow weight loss really is.

I was once a guest on the show "Penn and Teller: Bullshit". It was an excellent show about various things they were debunking. They did a segment on infomercials and interviewed an infomercial producer. What she said was that the people know they are selling bogus goods and making false claims about what their product(s) will do for you. They also know that they will get sued. They put a couple million dollars aside to pay for the law suits, and bank the rest of the millions that you happily paid them for the hope of quick, easy weight loss.

So next time you are tempted to buy that pill, protein powder, exercise device, magazine, supplement or hypnosis tape, remember you have to deficit 3,500 calories to lose a pound of fat. There are many snake oil sales folks out there willing to take your money and will happily tell you that you can lose 10 pounds in two days. You can, of course, lose water weight quickly but that isn't what we are after. We want real weight/fat loss that doesn't come straight back on as soon as we take in some sodium.

It is OK if you are stuck at a plateau. Learn to maintain that weight and get comfortable there. You can drop more later, but learning to maintain is crucial.

Learning Takes Time

I learned to swim when I was five. My Dad tried to teach me by throwing me in the water and yelling instructions at me and then getting upset when I sank. I was traumatized. I then went over to the kiddie pool, where my Mom was with my two little brothers, and she told me to get in the kiddie pool and float. I did and once I knew I could float, I could swim. I wasn't so afraid and thanks Mom for being gentle about it.

Weight maintenance is like learning to float. It won't necessarily get you to the other side of the pool, but you won't drown either. In fact, if you are able to maintain any weight below your top weight, you are successful. Remember to take credit for your successes, even if you haven't reached your goal and to celebrate the journey.

The journey to permanent weight control is fraught with both frustration and joy. Yes it is frustrating to have to stop along the path and wait the plateau out. Your ability to do just that is a large predictor of your ability to ultimately be a successful loser. If you can learn to enjoy the stops along the way, your journey will be that much more pleasant.

Life Gets in the Way

There are inevitably other challenges during the weight loss phase that must be tackled if one hopes to lose weight and keep it off. Life will throw you curve balls while you are working on your weight.

Wouldn't it be great if life stopped until you had your weight under control and then continued once you had a good handle on it? I think so. However, life isn't like that. The truth is even though this weight work takes time, energy and focus, it needs to happen in addition to everything else you have going on.

It is one thing to learn how to float in the kiddie pool and quite another to try and float in the ocean. Losing weight might feel like floating in the kiddie pool some of the time but once in awhile, life will throw you in the ocean. Learning to lose weight and keep it off requires navigating the ever changing waters of life and moderating your eating and exercise when life requires that of you.

Injuries and Illness

Often what I see is that people will be going along fine, losing weight and working out and then they sprain their ankle, get really sick, need to have surgery, etc... This means no working out for a period of time. Sometimes this is enough to send people back to square one. The ultimately successful losers will adjust their intake, find other forms of exercise they can still do until they heal, and realize this is but a temporary setback and not the end of the game.

Lonny was using exercise to an extreme amount to control his calories in/calories out equation. He had come to the clinic and been very successful at losing weight and with the amount of exercise he was doing, he was maintaining that loss. He had the time to walk about 8 miles a day. He burned just over 800 calories, five days a week, with his walking regimen. That totaled 4,000 calories a week burned in exercise that he then made up for by eating those 4,000 calories. This method of weight control worked for Lonny for two years until he hurt his knee.

When Lonny realized he couldn't walk for awhile he had a lot of adjusting to do. If he did nothing he would gain just over a pound a week. He was unwilling to do that but was also unable to cut the 4,000 calories out completely. What he did was problem solve. He figured that he would be back to walking and that this was temporary. He was able to cut his intake by 2,000 calories a week and found that he could still do some water exercise if he got in the pool. He was able to add in about 2,000 calories a week of water aerobics and only gained about a pound during his two months off from walking. He also realized that his exercise routine was a bit too much for his body, at his age. Lonny was in his late 50's.

Over time, Lonny has learned to fill up his life with work he loves and needs both the food and exercise less. He is now able to walk 4 miles a day, injury free, and moderate his intake so he can maintain a healthy weight. For Lonny, who has been heavy since early childhood, this weight loss/weight maintenance education has taken I6 years. He can now maintain his weight comfortably, but the struggle was long and hard. He would tell you it was worth it, in a heartbeat.

Exercise takes about six months to become a habit in one's life. If you have started exercising recently, and you get injured, the challenge is to keep on going as soon as possible.

Let's say you have been exercising for 5 months and you love it. You are working out at the gym 3 days a week and walking the other days. This has allowed you to burn an additional 2,400 calories a week. This calorie burn, plus the good feelings from the exercise, has helped you to maintain your weight loss and feel great about how you look.

Then, you are walking along and completely miss a step. Next thing you know you are on the ground with a sprained ankle, black and blue toes and skinned knees. Ouch! You go visit your doctor, just to make sure nothing is broken, and are told you have to keep your foot up for 2 weeks and take it easy.

This is when the illness/injury voice can start talking to you. She says, "So, all this hard work and it's all derailed now. You know you are going to gain weight back so why not just give up now. You can't do this."

She wants you to go back to your old ways and stay exactly as you were. Don't listen to her. Instead, get logical. If you are down for two weeks, it will not affect your weight a year from now. Start thinking long term when it comes to weight loss and weight maintenance. Tell the voice that for the next two weeks your body will be burning calories trying to heal and that you will adjust your intake accordingly. Then, as soon as possible, you will be back to your old exercise routine. Remember, this will not affect your weight a year from now.

The other part of the injury and/or illness challenge is the feeling of needing comfort during this time. If you were sick or injured as a child and your mother made you your favorite cake/ pie/macaroni and cheese/mashed potatoes/ice cream, etc... you are likely to want those foods right now. You are cued to eat by the circumstance and your old response kicks in. This is a very important part of the weight loss/maintenance learning process. Learning new responses to old experiences is what will ultimately get and keep you successful. When you get through this challenge, without using food, it goes into your bank of new, successful behaviors and you will remember that next time you get hurt and/or sick.

We are fragile beings and the reality is that you may get injured and or sick again in the future. Next time, you will be ready for it.

Routine Changes

Other life challenges include a change of routine for various reasons. If you lived close enough to walk to school and now your child is going to a school that you have to drive to, you lose those walking calories. Small changes like this can add up.

Gayle used to bike to work. When she changed jobs she could no longer bike and gained 20 lbs. She couldn't figure out where the weight came from until she realized that she hadn't replaced her bike riding with another form of exercise and yet had kept her calorie intake the same. When she did the math she realized that she in fact, earned the twenty pounds and was going to either have to add in exercise, reduce her caloric intake or carry an extra twenty pounds. Gayle opted to work out on her lunch hour and eat her lunch at her desk. It took 9 months for her to lose the twenty pounds.

Tom lost 150 lbs. by keeping records. He was a weight loss master in that he had kept the weight off for years by weighing himself, keeping records and exercising. Then Tom moved to a new city. He felt like he had conquered his weight and so gave up the records. What he found was that he was less active in this new location and lonely. He slowly started slipping into his old habits and the weight began to come back on. Tom was smart and caught it quickly and went right back to the records. He discovered that he was taking in more calories than he thought and burning less than he thought. That denial was causing him to add pounds. Once he faced it, Tom was able to get his weight back down and has been stable at his weight, in his new location, for 8 months.

Grief and Loss

Grief is unavoidable. You are progressing in your weight work and then you suffer a loss. Emma was 20 pounds overweight and working on it when her brother, with whom she was very close, died of AIDS. She couldn't deal with the emotions and so began to eat to comfort and numb herself. She gained 100 lbs. from grief eating and her brother is still dead. The food takes the edge off, in the moment, but then gives you lots more grief to deal with in the form of obesity.

Pam gained 130 lbs. after her mother died. She watched her fit and beautiful mother die of stomach cancer and waste away to nothing. Pam was always very close to her mother and after she died the only thing that helped was ice cream, and lots of it. It made her feel good in the moment she was eating it. Pam wasn't ready to lose weight and/or deal with the feelings around her mother's death for 25 years. She walked around in a heavy body, eating ice cream until something snapped and she decided to change.

While you are working on your weight you may experience a loss. People who don't use food to deal with their emotions feel sad, cry, talk to loved ones, write in a journal, seek counseling, draw, paint, exercise, read, watch TV, etc... If you experience a loss during the weight loss/plateau phase I look at it as a great opportunity to try new coping skills. If you always eat when you are upset, this will take time to change. As long as you continue to write everything down and get on the scale each morning, you will still be in the game even if you are having high calorie days and the weight has stopped coming off. Again, you will realize this is a temporary setback and not the end of the game.

But It's the Holidays

Social events tend to throw people off. The idea that they won't be able to eat everything they used to eat at the Easter party, Passover, X-mas, Thanksgiving, etc... can really make people want to run the other way. "How can I deprive myself of Grandma's special once a year Sour Cream Chocolate Chip Fudge Cake?" There is the irrational fear that we won't ever be able to eat it again. There is also the black and white thinking to work through. The idea that you can have a little, and write it down and count the calories, is something most dieters learn at some point. You don't have to deprive yourself, you just can't eat the whole thing.

One has to remember that there will always be holidays, birthdays, Mother's Days, and random social gatherings to which you will be invited and there will most likely be food present. Sometimes the gathering will be all about food, think Thanksgiving. You have to learn to manage these events in order to be successful at keeping the weight off long term. When you commit to counting calories and writing down what you eat, you will learn to navigate high calorie social events by choosing exactly what you want to spend your calories on. If you have a high calorie day, here and there, it won't throw your weight off. It is what you do on average, over time, that determines your weight.

Chapter 4 Exercises:

1. Find a new way to reward yourself for a job well done. If you have always used food as a reward, take some time to come up with new ideas. Some ideas for rewards are: new clothes in your new size, a massage for every 5 pounds you lose, a magazine you wouldn't normally buy, a day off, etc…

2. Keep your eye on the goal. Write down your goal, tell someone, stay focused. It is easy to lose momentum now.

3. Add in exercise if you haven't already. If you can walk, you can walk around the block today. Tomorrow try for two blocks, etc…

4. Make a list of all the good things you have already received by losing weight.

5. Make a list of new coping skills you can try next time you experience a loss.

6. Imagine progressing past the plateau and getting to your goal.

5

Stage Five
Getting to Goal

THE DAY I REACHED MY goal weight, I cried. It was the same feeling I had when I finished the marathon. It was such an important goal for me to reach and was very hard won. Seeing l33 lbs. on the scale was like winning the lottery. After 4 months of a medically supervised liquid diet, I had lost all the weight I needed to lose. There is no better feeling and no food tastes even close to that good.

My feelings of accomplishment and pride were tinged with anxiety however. The fear that I wouldn't be able to maintain the weight loss was never far away. I also felt everyone on the side lines, who had watched me lose it, waiting and watching to see if I would gain it back.

I began keeping very obsessive food records and counting the calories. To maintain 133 lbs. I needed to take in 1,330 calories a day. If I exercised, I could eat a bit more, but that was it. When I began the medically supervised liquid diet, and was at my top weight, I had been taking in about 2,000 calories a day. The fast, though medically supervised and safe, didn't teach me how to live for a 133 lb. person. I learned how to drink 800 calories a day of liquid food, but I had no idea how to maintain that weight loss once I got down to my goal weight. I had to learn that once I got to goal and began eating again. This was very hard and I ended up gaining some of the weight back at first. I went all the way back up to 150 lbs. (not my top weight but getting up there) before I was able to cut my food calories and bring it back down. This was a very difficult period of time for me. To watch that hard won battle slipping away was painful.

The Honeymoon

Rona decided to lose weight as a 50th birthday gift to herself. She was very successful during the weight loss phase and went straight down to her goal weight of 120 lbs. She looked great, she felt great and for the first time in a very long time, she liked how she looked. Rona got so much praise and support for her dramatic weight loss that she was in a honeymoon period.

When you lose weight, people you barely know will comment on it. On the one hand, we wish our struggle wasn't so public; on the other hand, we get a lot of praise when we are winning the battle. Once you get down to your goal weight, or near it, you will be on a high. If you haven't been at this weight for quite some time, you will be marveling at what you can wear now, what size, what styles, how people treat you, etc...

You will happily be adjusting to sitting differently, eating differently and test driving your new body. This period can be exciting and thrilling. The high of the new you can carry you through the early phase of weight maintenance.

When I lost weight the praise was constant. From my family members to the guy at Starbucks, people were very vocal. "You look fantastic, how much have you lost?" "How did you do it?

You look great." "OMG, I haven't seen you in so long and you just look fabulous. Have you lost weight?" This feedback is very motivating and can help you keep your calories low and keep the exercise going.

Shelly was on a high for months after she lost weight. She had been heavy since she was a child and for the first time in her adult life, got down to a size 12. She marveled at what she could wear, how small the clothes looked, how she had to move her seat up in her car to accommodate her new size, how she could cross her legs, wear heels, etc... Since Shelly is a nurse practioner for an ob/gyn, she would see people once a year for their pap smears. Her day was comprised of one person after another commenting on how they didn't even recognize her from the Shelly they had seen last year.

During this phase you will need to continue to keep food records and weigh yourself regularly. The successful losers continue to monitor themselves in some way for years after they have lost their weight.

Fear of Success

I can't tell you how many times I have worked with people who get really close to their goal and then start to freak out. They start having thoughts like, "What will I do when I get there? I know how to lose weight but I've never maintained a weight loss before. What if I can't do it this time either?" This is anxiety talking. This fear of success can be enough to cause people to either gain some weight back and/or just not quite reach the goal weight they had set for themselves.

If you get close and then turn back in the other direction you could be suffering from fear of success. We think we are all afraid to fail, but a large number of people are truly afraid to let themselves have what they want and be happy.

This is a time to get some support if you need it. Either in a group or even better in individual therapy so you can work through these fears and allow yourself to not only reach your goal, but enjoy it at the same time.

Adjusting To the New You

Just as we didn't realize how fat we were, we won't be able to tell how thin we have become. This is a good thing to know so you're not disappointed when you get to goal. Our self image is something that may never change even though our bodies have.

I have been thin for 20 years and yet even writing the sentence now makes me uncomfortable. Calling myself thin is still strange after all these years. Since I was the "fat" girl, or the chubby one, that is still my sense of myself. I know logically that I am not fat now, but emotionally I'm still the fat girl.

Recently someone told me that I looked as though I'd never had a weight problem. That still shocks me. Not long ago, when I was at a food addiction conference, and told someone that I used to be heavy, she didn't believe me. That shocked me too. When one of my clients told me that I looked like a runner, I thought she was kidding.

This is still my reaction even though I have heard these comments for 20 years. So, don't expect to get thin and suddenly feel like it's you. That has happened for a few people I've met but it is the exception and not the rule!

Knowing this might happen can help you keep your weight down. It can take years for our self image to change and it may never do so. The problem arises when we feel like we want to go back to looking as we did, since we still think we look that way anyway.

This is a good time to have photos taken of you, once again. When we see ourselves in photos, we can't deny what we look like. This and shopping for clothes is good too as we can see what size we now wear, even if we think we are still fat. When I can now pick out a size 6, and sometimes even a size 4, I know logically I am not still fat.

The Honeymoon is Over

Once you have maintained your weight loss for awhile, and maybe even gained a few pounds back, the high will start to wear off. People will get used to you at your new weight and the compliments will taper off. This tends to happen right around the time you are getting sick of having to work so hard to keep what you have earned.

After maintaining her weight loss for about six months, Rona began to gain some weight back. She gained about 15 pounds and the compliments stopped. She could no longer wear her smallest size clothing and she felt defeated. This is a dangerous point on the weight loss journey. Weight regain, if not handled well, can send some people all the way back to their top weight and even higher.

At the obesity clinic, we have a saying that goes, "You haven't really worked the program until you have gained some weight back and worked it back down." You not only have to work the weight back down, but you also have to deal with the feelings that tend to come along with weight regain. Those feelings can include: shame, depression, feeling like a failure, etc... If you expect this to happen, your chances of navigating it are much better than if you go into the weight loss experience thinking you will be one of the few who never gains a pound back. Learning to work your weight back down after gaining a few pounds back is a vital part of learning how to keep your weight off for good.

No matter how much understanding we have of the process of weight loss, and weight maintenance, there is still the feeling that we should be done by now. We have lost all this weight, why is it still so hard?

Shelly also started to come down from her high after maintaining her weight for about 9 months. She realized the compliments were tapering off. She was beginning to get used to the fact that she could wear a size 12 and so was everyone else. Although there were still patients coming in who hadn't seen her in a year and were marveling at her, it began to happen less and less. This began the end of the honeymoon phase for Shelly.

Honeymoon is over voice can start talking to you now. It says things like, "Ah, you look good enough. You don't have to keep up all this work. You deserve a (fill in the blank of a high calorie food you love)." This is the lazy, tired voice (that we all have to one degree or another). It would like you to be able to coast rather than exert effort to stay thin. This part of us also forgets how miserable we were at our top weight.

To deal with honeymoon is over voice, you have to learn to appreciate your new body every day. You have to remind yourself of how you looked, and felt, at your top weight. You need to remember how much better you look and feel now. You also have to learn that you deserve to look and feel your best and the effort it takes to do that is worth it and better than giving in to an impulse in the moment.

It is helpful to think of putting this voice to sleep and throwing a blanket over it. That way, if it does talk in its sleep, the blanket will muffle the sound.

Reality Sets In

The timing of this is very individual but usually happens somewhere between six months to a year and a half into maintenance. At this point the high of the weight loss phase is over and the honeymoon, complete with constant compliments, is over as well. Now the daily task of writing down the food, counting calories, trying hard to keep the calories in/calories out in the range that will allow you to maintain your weight loss becomes a little more tedious.

This is the time to make peace with the work that it will take to keep you at your goal. When honeymoon is over voice tells you to eat the hot fudge sundae, you can. We know we can have the sundae, write it down and work the calories into our day; however, it may just be that slippery slope. The old behavior of using food as reward will need to change, or the type of food you use, or the weight will begin to come back. Working your maintenance is really about gaining and losing a small amount of weight, over and over again. I've never met anyone who stayed exactly the same weight, everyday, for life.

Lorna, one of my patients, had lost 185 lbs. She was thrilled! It was the first time, since she could remember that she felt good in her body. At 62, carrying that much weight, was taking such a toll on her body that she could barely walk. 185 lbs. lighter, she could run. She could also buy normal sized clothing and was ecstatic about looking and feeling better. Her weight had kept her from living a full life and now, her life was full!

Of all the patients I have worked with, I didn't expect what happened to happen with Lorna down the road. She happily maintained her weight, within a 10 lb. range, for two years. About the time people start to find it easier and get a real handle on what it takes to keep the weight off.

One of the behaviors Lorna never put into play was keeping food records. She was just not motivated enough to do that. So, slowly, the weight started creeping back on. First it was 20 lbs., then 25, then 45….She is now up 100 lbs. She is still maintaining her 85 lb. loss, which is great, but with the added weight, her physical problems are returning. It's becoming harder for her to walk, she has had to go back and buy larger sized clothing (she gave away all her fat clothes) and she has begun to go back to the smaller life she was living as a large person.

Lorna is still in the game though and still weighing herself everyday. She has just lost control of her eating. As I write, she has agreed to start keeping records, so perhaps she will be able to turn the gaining around at this point. Even if she can maintain at this weight she is much better off than she was.

Lorna got comfortable at her lower weight and then she got lazy. She stopped bringing her lunch to work and started eating out more. She also started turning to food for comfort when she got stressed, like she used to. During her weight loss, and initial maintenance, she kept her house clean of dangerous food. Those foods had found their way back in. All these things came together to cause the 100 lb. regain. Add the shame and humiliation factor, after so much praise was heaped on her for such a successful loss, and Lorna was really down.

It's hard to deal with weight regain, but it's just a part of the journey.

Finding New Rewards

If you used food to reward yourself in the past, now is the time to change that behavior and develop new ways to reward yourself. The same holds true if you were using food to cope with boredom, sadness, loneliness, grief, anger, happiness, frustration, etc... Using food to deal with any of the above makes no logical sense. It's like saying, "My car is out of gas, I think I'll go get my hair done." The hairdo might make you feel good for the moment but it won't do anything to take care of the fact that you need to put gas in your car. It is just a distraction. Food is a self-destructive distraction.

Your goal now is to find new and better ways of dealing with the issues that come up in your life. It is helpful to write down the various reasons you turn to food, when you are not hungry, and come up with your own new solutions to those situations.

For example, if you eat out of boredom when you are home, have fun and interesting things to do at home that don't involve food. Some ideas are: jigsaw puzzles, art/craft projects, home improvement (like painting or cleaning), reading, writing, internet surfing, cleaning out drawers or closets, etc... Come up with your own list and stock your house with fun things to do. It's worth the effort!

Chapter 5 Exercises:

1. Find a non-food way to reward yourself for a job well done.

2. Pick something you love that doesn't have calories and give it to yourself as a weight loss reward.

3. Keep your biggest pants, dress, and suit and put them on occasionally. This will remind you of how far you've come and why you want to keep it up.

4. Have a picture taken of your entire body. This will help you see the weight loss. If you have one at your top weight it is fun to compare.

5. Add in something new that makes you happy. If you were using the food to make you happy, make a list of alternatives and add at least one a month.

6

Stage Six
Learning to Stay There

THIS IS ONE OF THE most, if not the most, important stages of the weight loss/weight maintenance journey. Learning to keep the weight off is the key to success. No one wants to lose a lot of weight, get all the compliments, enjoy the new body only to turn around and gain it all back. This is not what anyone wants and yet it happens all the time. I believe it's because people get thrown off by how hard maintenance can be. They weren't expecting it. The difficulty encountered now often sends people all the way back to square one. Don't let that happen to you. Know that to maintain a weight loss will be work. It is the same work you did to get there only you get to do it in a thinner body.

Who Maintains a Weight Loss?

The million dollar question is: "Who are the successful long term losers and what sets them apart from everyone else?"

The patients I have worked with have taught me a lot about what it takes and who can do this work. There was a recent study published that said the successful long term losers had a stronger impulse control center in the brain than those who could not sustain the weight loss. It also showed those of us with weight problems have brains that are very turned on by food. This was true both for the people who could not maintain the loss and for those who could. The amount of time the loss was maintained didn't seem to affect the extent to which the brain was turned on by food.

We still don't know too much about this aspect of weight control, but what I have observed over the years tells me several things that are unique to the weight loss masters.

None of them went on a crazy diet and then went off it. Not one. They all were eating healthy and keeping track in some way. They were either keeping food records and/or weighing themselves daily. They also had a change in their mindsets. They thought, "I am now a person who eats this way and exercises." Not one of them looked at this as a temporary fix. It was a permanent lifestyle change.

The clients I can predict will regain their weight don't keep food records. They might maintain it for awhile, but without those records they don't keep the bulk of it off. The old eating habits don't go away. They might go to sleep for awhile, but they can come back in a heartbeat.

The others who will put weight back on make the mistake of not getting on the scale everyday. Yes, everyday. If you do that, you will never see a 20 pound weight gain. If you don't, you are at risk of losing control.

How Long Does This Take?

When the weight loss masters were studied, they found that there were a few predictors of weight regain in successful losers.

Apparently, the first two years of weight maintenance are crucial. Successful losers, who were able to maintain their loss for two years, were generally successful at keeping it off after that. Most of the weight regain happened in those crucial couple of years. This is extremely important to understand. If you think about it in terms of how long you have been overweight, and on or off diets, then you will get a better idea of how long it might take to get it under control. Not to say that if you were overweight for 35 years, it will take another 35 to conquer it. However, if you have been overweight for 35 years, you won't have it handled after 6 months or one year. Give yourself lots of time to adjust to the changes you are making. It's not easy, but it is worth it.

Of the people I studied, 25% were able to maintain their weight loss for 3 years or more. I asked them if they found it got easier with time. 70% of them said yes, it does get easier the longer you are able to keep the weight off. 30%, even though they were successful at losing weight and keeping it off for 3, or more, years said it was still a struggle and they needed to be constantly awake and aware!

What Is Weight Maintenance?

When we think of keeping the weight off, we often think of maintaining the exact same weight, on a daily basis, for life. This is not what weight maintenance really looks like. Weight maintenance is really about gaining and losing small amounts of weight, all the time. In other words, most people have a weight range in which they live. If you have lost a large amount of weight, it is good to keep this range rather small. Some people will allow themselves to gain 3 to 5 pounds and then work their weight back down.

When people who have lost a lot of weight allow themselves to gain more than 10% of their weight back, over the first year, it was not a good sign. The first two years of weight maintenance are critical in predicting long term success. Those who did regain more than 10% of their weight back were very unlikely to get their weight back down to their original goal weight.

This suggests that vigilance during that crucial 2 year period will pay off down the road. On the other hand, it would also lead one to believe that falling off the wagon in those early days is a sign that one will not be successful. Knowing this puts you that much ahead of most dieters.

Coping With Emotional Eating During Maintenance

When I lost weight, and got to my goal, I was very focused on staying there. It was a hard won fight and I was intent on keeping my weight down. In order to do that, I had to confront my tendency to use food as a drug. My old behavior was to use food when I was upset, angry, lonely, bored, frustrated, happy, etc…

Soon after I had gotten down to my goal weight I had a clear experience of emotionally reaching for food. At the time I was single and dating. I was dating someone who really wasn't good for me and wasn't all that nice. He did or said something hurtful while we were on the phone. When I hung up, I knew I was upset. The next thing I knew I was standing in front of the refrigerator reaching for some low-fat cupcakes. I stood there in front of the open fridge, cupcakes in hand and said,

"Are you reaching for this food because you are upset about

what just happened on the phone?"

"Yes," the answer was clear.

"Are you going to eat this anyway?"

"Yes."

So I ate the cupcake, only instead of eating a dozen, I ate one. I wrote it down and wrote the calories down too. After I was done, I asked myself,

"OK, did eating that cupcake help you with your relationship issue?"

"Well, no but it made me feel better in the moment."

So I learned clearly that the food doesn't solve the real problem but in the moment does a good job of both distracting me and taking the edge off by increasing my brain levels of dopamine. The brain chemicals are powerful and why we think certain foods are addictive. The same chemicals are produced in the brain when we eat the high fat/salt/sugar foods, that are produced when we take in drugs of abuse.

Emotional eating comes into play any time you USE food as a drug to deal with your feelings. It is vital that we acknowledge the power of food. When we are actually eating and feeling the pleasure of that, it can help us tune out our problems. The difficulty though is that it doesn't actually do anything to fix the problem and if we overeat consistently, we create a new problem by adding excess weight.

By keeping food records, asking yourself if you are actually hungry before you eat anything and by acknowledging the power of the food to give you momentary pleasure, you can work through your tendency to use food for emotional comfort.

I can happily tell you that after years of maintaining my weight, I don't use food that way anymore. I still get pleasure from eating but when I am upset I no longer find myself in front of the fridge looking for love. I have learned to call a friend, write about my feelings, feel them and address the reason for them. Take control of the things I can control and let go of the rest. I have learned to acknowledge it is OK to feel badly sometimes. We are not always supposed to be happy. Life just isn't like that. There are ups and downs and it is OK to experience the downs, just as it is OK to fully experience the ups.

If you can't completely stop eating for emotional reasons, then you can learn to maintain your weight loss by using lower calorie foods. You can bargain with emotional eating if you can't completely stop the behavior. It is especially difficult if you have been eating emotionally for many, many years. You can eat a lot of fruit, veggies, Cindy's choice is sugar-free Jell-O with Cool Whip, air popped popcorn, etc... and still not eat too many calories. Is it best not to use food at all? Sure it is, however that is not always possible. You can still maintain your weight loss and use food occasionally.

When Cindy got down to her goal weight, after gaining and losing over 100 lbs. several times, she was intent on staying there. She will tell me, even after maintaining her weight for seven years, that sometimes she still uses food emotionally. The difference now is that she will choose lower calorie foods. Those foods still give her pleasure and distract her from her problems, but with less destructive results.

Weight Regain

Ah, the nastiest of all weight loss demons. Weight regain can seemingly come out of nowhere. It shows up when we fall asleep at the wheel of our weight work. Even if we get a bit drowsy, it can appear.

Weight regain needs to be expected so you can work with it. If you think, like I did, that you will never gain a pound back and you will be perfect, then weight regain can take you down. It's like deciding you don't need to learn self-defense because nothing will ever happen to you. Hopefully, nothing ever will, but if it does it is best to be prepared.

Learning to fight constantly is what successful weight maintenance is all about. The more times you are able to work a small gain back down, the more successful you will be long term. For Lorna, with 100 lbs. back, she is finding it very difficult to keep fighting.   If you can keep weight regain in check, when you have only gained a couple of pounds back, then you have an excellent chance of maintaining your weight loss long term.

The Apple

The apple that caused a 100 lb. weight gain is a famous story at the obesity clinic where I work. A patient there, who was on the liquid fast, broke down and ate an apple. He had been fasting for months, had lost over l00 lbs., and was doing great when he saw a beautiful apple. He just had to have it and ate it. He was not at his goal yet and intended to keep fasting. He was just going to have this one apple and get right back on the fast.

The problem was, the apple had more sodium than what he had been taking in and so it caused him to gain 5 pounds of water weight. When he came back to clinic to weigh in and the scale was up he freaked out. Since he didn't understand that it was water and that in fact he had lost weight that week that would show up later, he just left the program completely.

About a year later he came back 100 pounds heavier than when he had left. He had gained all the weight back. He was ashamed and upset. What he didn't understand, he has since had to learn while he works the weight back down, was that calories in/calories out doesn't always work out perfectly when you would like it to. If he had known that, the 5 lbs. of water weight would not have caused him to gain the next 95 lbs.

Our bodies are not machines and hence they don't always behave in the way we would like. If you know this, you won't be so thrown off by the water weight swings that happen to all of us. Knowing this will help you keep a 100 calorie apple from turning into a 100 lb. weight gain.

You'll Get Paid Later

Lucy was mad. She had lost weight but according to her records, she should still be losing more. "This is just wrong," she would say with feeling. To make sure, she went and had her thyroid checked and it was fine.

According to the labeling laws we currently have in place, the food companies get a 10 % leeway in either direction. In other words, they can say their food has 10% less calories than it actually does. I'm pretty sure they take advantage of this. So when you are counting the calories of a food with a label, you would be smart to add 10%. If the label says that cupcake is 100 calories, it is probably really 110 calories. That may not seem like much but if you add that amount to the other packaged foods you eat, you can see how it might throw your record keeping off.

The other issue Lucy was dealing with was water weight.

Just like the man with the apple, water weight is the bane of many dieters existence and a nasty dragon to slay. Lucy was taking in enough to lose and yet her body would sometimes even go up a couple of pounds. Knowing this was water weight, Lucy was able to keep going. She was able to understand that she was in fact losing fat and would get paid on the scale later.

When we work hard and are able to pull off a low calorie day, we want results now. We want to get on that scale the next morning and see the pay off. When we don't, it can be frustrating and disheartening. Learning to deal with these feelings, and keep going anyway, is vital in learning to keep the weight off long term.

Gaining Weight Successfully

Part of learning to keep weight off, is learning how to handle inevitable weight gains. We have a phrase at the obesity clinic that we use regularly. We say, "Overeating is normal and inevitable." What we mean by this is that no one eats exactly the same thing, everyday for life. There will be times, even for naturally thin people, when you will take in more calories than you burn and gain some weight.

The trick here is to know this ahead of time and have tools to deal with it before it goes very far. Most weight loss masters give themselves a weight range that they feel comfortable with. If their weight goes up higher than the top of their range, they go back to the behaviors they know worked for them when they were losing. They will return to keeping food records, if they had stopped doing that, and will attempt to string 2 or 3 low calorie days together so that they see the weight go back down.

When you only let yourself have a 2 or 3 pound weight range, this can help keep overeating to a minimum. This also makes it relatively easy to get back down to the weight you like to be at. It's when we let it go longer, and are looking at a ten pound (or more) weight gain, that it can get daunting.

Keep your weight range small and take the small gains in stride. If you have been continuing to monitor your weight daily, this is possible. It is when you stop paying attention that the regain can become a real problem. Stay awake and aware. You have worked too hard to let it go.

Tracking Your Weight

Some people will get obsessed with weighing themselves and get on the scale multiple times a day. This is generally a negative experience. Our daily weight fluctuations are not at all important in the big picture. In fact, they will tend to make people a little crazy as some of the ups and downs make no logical sense. Once a day, in the morning, first thing, is the best way to go. It will give you the truest picture of what is happening.

During early weight maintenance, keeping close tabs on your weight is vital. As we discussed in Chapter 3, daily (once a day first thing) weighing is best. You should write down the weight, along with your calories in/out, and then average the weight for the week. For example, Sally's weights for the week were 130, 132, 131, 131, 131.5, 131, and 133. When we average Sally's weekly weights we get 131.3 lbs. This is the truest picture of what she actually weighs. If she had only weighed on the day the scale said 133, she would have been upset. If she had weighed only on the day she was 130, she would have been thrilled but then really upset if she was doing well and then got on the scale to see 133. "What a minute, I was just 130 and I have been eating low calorie and exercising. This is not fair!"

When people get very frustrated, they tend to give up. We don't want this. We want to be able to understand what is happening and then work with it to get what we want. We want to track our weight in a way that gives us a clear picture, doesn't send us running back in the other direction, and keeps us moving forward. If you weigh yourself everyday, from now on, you will never see a 20 lb. weight gain that came from nowhere. Over time you will begin to notice things like, when you eat chips, the scale goes up the next day (water weight). Or perhaps your monthly cycle will cause a water weight gain. Keeping track will alert you to these patterns and allow you to understand them vs. freak out over them. Knowledge is power.

A Living Weight

Sometimes, one has to accept that maintaining a super low weight just isn't going to happen. You may have gotten down to a weight that you haven't seen since high school during the weight loss phase. This is very exciting and sometimes maintainable. However, often when the honeymoon phase ends, your ability to maintain that weight does too.

A living weight is one that you can maintain, without going crazy. You want to find a balance between your weight work and enjoying life. If trying to maintain a super low weight is too hard, it will make you miserable. A living weight, on the other hand, is one you can be comfortable maintaining, with effort, but not superhuman effort. It should continue to be work, but not

Herculean work. No one can maintain that long term, except maybe Hercules. Figuring out a good living weight takes some time to accept and to learn.

For example, I would love to weigh 124 lbs. I am 5'7" and have achieved that weight at various times. It is my lowest adult weight and I like the way I feel and look at that weight. However, I can't maintain it without keeping my calories really low and exercising constantly. I had to accept that and be happy maintaining at 130 lbs. I'm much happier this way and have learned to love and accept myself here.

Once you find a living weight, and learn to like it, you are well on your way to lifetime maintenance. It's a journey, and a process.

Make Lists and Look at Them Regularly

This is a good time to make a list of why you began to lose weight in the first place. As the difficulty of daily weight work sets in, it is easy to lose sight of why you wanted to lose weight to begin with. Make a list of what got you going on your weight loss journey. That painful moment in the mirror, in the photo, the store window where you saw just how big you were is good to keep in mind.

Tammy was so heavy at her top weight that she needed to use handicapped restrooms because she was afraid she would get stuck in the smaller ones. She was so afraid that she wouldn't fit in the bathroom in the plane that she once went all the way to Europe, a ten hour flight, without going to the bathroom. She drank nothing and held it the entire way.

As your weight goes up, and you get bigger, your life tends to get smaller. Just as Tammy was afraid to get stuck in a bathroom,

Cindy was afraid to put herself out there in the dating world at her top weight. She was alone and lonely but too ashamed of her size and appearance to go out and meet men. Lorna was too afraid to go on the train with her grandchildren because she knew how small the aisles and the bathrooms on trains are. She decided not to go just to be safe and missed a wonderful trip.

Make a list of all the things you can do now that you are thinner. Some examples my clients have shared are: shop in normal stores, run, hike, travel with ease, sit on the floor and play with kids, wear a belt, tie shoes, etc...

Chapter 6 Exercises:

1. Give yourself credit for what you have accomplished. Losing weight and working on keeping it off are two of the hardest and best things you can do for yourself. Congratulate yourself on getting this far.

2. Repeat this mantra when the going gets tough, "The first two years are the hardest. The first two years are the hardest....." Know that it will get easier with time and that the rewards will still be as wonderful.

3. Expect some weight gain. This is normal and inevitable. It may be 2 pounds or 10, but if you expect it and learn to work it back down, you can keep it off for good.

4. Believe that you can do this. If others have been able to, you can too.

7

Stage Seven
Accepting That It Is a
Life Long Journey

So YOU HAVE LOST WEIGHT and either gotten to your goal, or maybe somewhere close to it. Congratulations. There are few things in life that feel as good, look as good, or give us such a sense of accomplishment. It is very important that you take credit for your success and enjoy it. Now the real work begins. Lifetime maintenance is something you will need to focus on, and work on, for life.

There has been a shift recently towards the idea that weight maintenance is its own journey. The weight loss phase has its own dragons to slay but it is only a small part of the ultimate journey of keeping the weight off. No one wants to navigate the weight loss phases successfully only to put the weight back on and have to go through it all again.

Cindy has lost over 150 pounds, 6 times. She started getting heavy around age 11 and battled her weight her whole life until about 6 years ago. 8 years ago, in desperation, Cindy had bariatric surgery to help her control her weight. The surgery did help her because she couldn't eat as much at once but she still found ways to gain weight by eating less more often.

After gaining 50 pounds back of her 150 pound loss, even

after the surgery, Cindy began to learn about calories, portion sizes, exercise and how to keep food records. She became a diligent record keeper and has since been able to bring her weight down to its lowest since she was 11 and Cindy is now 66. She had to accept that due to the severity of her problem she will most likely need to keep records the rest of her life. She is fine with that considering it has helped her maintain her weight loss and that is something she was never able to do before. She was great at losing and gaining but maintaining was another animal completely.

Cindy also had to make peace with her current body. When you lose and gain large amounts of weight, the skin may have a problem shrinking along with you. This can be very upsetting when you have done so much hard work, gotten down to a nice, healthy weight and yet still don't look good. Hanging skin cannot be lost by dieting and the only option is plastic surgery. Cindy was fortunate that she could afford surgery and after maintaining her weight loss for over 3 years, she decided to have the skin removed. Now, at 66, she looks and feels better than she ever has. She is out there dancing, dating and enjoying life. She gets great joy in being able to move around with ease. She has also discovered the joy of shopping for clothes. When she was heavy, clothes shopping was a necessary evil. Now it is fun and joyous. It took her a long time not to head for the larger sizes, but after years of weight maintenance, she now feels comfortable shopping among the regular sizes. She would tell you that no food, no binge, ever felt as good as she does now. Does she sometimes miss the food? Yes she does. Does she ever have high calorie days and overeat? Absolutely. Will she ever go back up 150 lbs.? Never.

Maintenance is Boring

I am sorry to have to tell you this, but maintenance can be really boring. When you compare it to the thrill of losing weight, the honeymoon phase with your new body and all the compliments you get at first, the maintenance phase has little applause attached to it. It's a quiet thing and a daily thing.

Rachel lost over 100 pounds by exercising and counting calories. As I mentioned previously, she had to decide that she was now a person who eats well and exercises as opposed to thinking of herself as being on a diet or doing this exercise thing just so she can lose the weight. She had to accept that these behaviors that she was doing to get to goal needed to continue if she was going to stay there.

Since Rachel didn't do a drastic diet she was basically living for the 125 lb. person she became. By taking in and burning enough calories to weigh 125 lbs. while she was losing, Rachel only had to continue what she was doing to stay there. Since it took her a long time to lose the weight, she had a lot of practice maintaining it by the time she finally got there. This is the best way to lose weight and ease into maintenance.

The data from the National Weight Control Registry is clear. Of those they surveyed who had lost an average of 66 pounds and maintained that loss for just over 5 years, the women reported taking in about 1,300 calories a day and the men 1,685 per day. On average they were getting just under 25% of their calories from fat. This is what they did, on average, and it is what allowed them to be successful. Knowing this is what it takes to maintain a significant weight loss is helpful. It makes the facts very clear that we cannot go back to our old ways and expect to keep the weight off. Accepting this is crucial, and continuing to do it is what sets the successful maintainers apart from the weight regainers.

When we forget where we came from and begin to take our new weight for granted, the tedious nature of the weight work can get to us. This is the boring phase of maintenance, when the weight work can get dull. Dull voice says things like, "You know, you look great, you feel great, so why not let yourself enjoy that cake right now. You've earned it. You deserve it."

Never Forget Where You Came From

Since I work in the field, I am around people all the time who are trying to lose weight and are miserable in their current bodies. This is a constant reminder to me of how happy I am to be able to be in a slender body and maintain it easily, and how horrible it was to be fat and uncomfortable. Keeping this in the forefront of your mind can be a great tool to help you stay focused. Some of my clients will keep their fat pictures, a fat outfit, something from their "before" self to remind them of how far they have come.

Michael keeps a pair of his big pants and when he is having a hard time with his weight work, he will put them on. He says he could probably fit two of the current Michaels into those pants. Shelly kept her fat pants too and was trying to put them on one day and by accident found out that she could fit her entire body into one leg. This was helpful to her and a great reminder of how things were.

Tammy says she got her life back. That as she was getting bigger and bigger, her world was getting smaller and smaller. She was to the point where she was too big to move much and would just stay home and eat. Now that she has lost 80 pounds, she moves more, goes out, has friends and has even flown to Europe with no fear of getting stuck in the bathroom on the plane. When Tammy gets sick of working on her weight she remembers how it was and that keeps her going.

The Good News

According to the NWCR study, and my own experience and research, maintaining a weight loss gets easier over time for most people. The first two years being the hardest, and then it gradually gets easier, so that less effort is needed to stay the same weight. Even better news is that the pleasure of maintaining your healthy body at its lower weight, doesn't decrease. So the work gets easier and the rewards stay the same. Doesn't that sound good?

Although, for 30% of the people I surveyed, they had to continue to struggle somewhat to maintain their loss. One of them said, "It's like an annoying part-time job."

When I first got down to my goal weight, I was scared. I didn't know if I'd be able to maintain it and was told by so many, "Oh, you'll just gain it back." I practiced the behaviors I knew would work and didn't give up. I kept meticulous food records. I exercised a lot, and weighed myself everyday. Even with all that in place, I still gained some weight back. I had a hard time keeping my calories down. It took me several years to get my weight back down and keep it there. Now, after maintaining my weight since 1990, I no longer have to keep food records. My eating and exercise habits are in place and my weight is stable without a lot of effort. I still weigh myself everyday, as do most of the weight loss masters, but my eating and exercise I no longer have to track.

Sometimes Life Gangs Up on You

Part of learning how to keep weight off for the long term is learning how to deal with the curves life will throw at you, without overeating. If overeating was always your coping mechanism in the past, then it can be very hard to develop new ones. This also gets easier with time and practice but sometimes we get hit with too much at once.

Shelly was doing very well at maintaining her weight. She gave herself a 5 pound range and when she was inching up toward the top of her range, she'd go back to her vigilant behaviors. By that I mean she would: keep excellent food records, make sure her calories were low and exercise. She would also "clean up" her food choices. Shelly loved to eat cake, cookies, crackers, French fries, etc... When she needed to get her weight back down she would forgo all these treats and stick to vegetables, fruits, lean protein and some whole grains.

Just as Shelly was getting the hang of maintenance, after 3 years of working at it, she got hit with several tough things at once. First, she learned that she needed knee replacement surgery. Even though Shelly was now at a comfortable weight, she had been morbidly obese her entire life. That had taken a permanent toll on her knees and without the surgery she would not be able to walk. Her knee joint was bone on bone and the pain was excruciating.

In order to have the surgery, which she did and it was successful, she had to go on blood thinning medication to prevent the risk of developing a post-op clot. While on the medication she couldn't eat many of the fruits and vegetables she would always turn to, to get her weight back down. This really threw her off. Never in her years of maintenance had anyone ever told her not to eat fruits and vegetables.

Then the surgery was much more intense and painful than she was prepared for. The rehabilitation process was slow and also very painful. This meant that she was unable to work for a period of time. Shelly loves her work. It not only fills up her time, but makes her feel good. This meant her routine had to change. We talked about routine changes earlier and how they can throw off your weight work. We also covered how illness and injury can throw you off track. Shelley had both of these issues to deal with.

While she was working on attacking these issues, her beloved Aunt passed away. So now she also had grief and loss thrown in the mix. She was overwhelmed.

What Shelly did was just accept that this was going to be a rough patch, both physically and emotionally. She made it her goal to not lose any weight, but to do her best to keep her weight where it was. Rather than set unrealistic goals at this time in her life, she just attempted to maintain her weight, at the high end of her range, knowing that all of this was temporary and she would have her normal life back soon.

She did what she could exercise-wise and found that she was able to do pool aerobics, which she also enjoyed. She was able to keep food records and even without her favorite fruits and vegetables was able to keep her calories within reason. She did this by making sure there was nothing "dangerous" in her house. No high calorie, processed food that she was likely to overeat.

She also worked on her new coping skills. She shared about

her pain in her weekly support group and accepted the group's support and sympathy. That helped her tremendously. She also reached out to the few "safe" people in her life who understood what she was going through.

Shelly used her time to make lists of what motivated her to lose weight in the first place. She wrote down her experience of giving the pap smear to the woman who was her same height and weight and how painful it was to see herself mirrored back in this woman. She wrote down the time she thought she looked spectacular and then saw a photo of that event and couldn't believe how fat she was. Her triggering events.

She then made lists of all the benefits of being thinner. She could move more easily and she got so many compliments from people who were supportive of her. She wrote down the time she cried in the Nordstrom's dressing room because she had accidentally put on a pair of pants and fit into one leg. She had pulled her old size without thinking about it and was so overcome with joy, that she cried.

Shelly has accepted that this is a lifelong journey and that she will never be "done" with it. Although she doesn't like that, she has come to terms with it and when life throws curves at her, she deals with them and, so far, she is winning!

But I'm Still Not Thin

I hear this often from people who have lost weight. They may have lost a lot of weight but can't see it. I am one of those people. Just as I was surprised at photos of myself at my top weight, I am still surprised at photos of myself now at this weight. I have been at this weight, give or take five pounds, for 19 years (not including pregnancy) and yet when someone refers to me as thin, I'm still surprised. I am 5'7" and weigh 130 lbs. so logically I know that I am no longer fat, but I don't call myself thin either.

This is good to know upfront so you don't feel disappointed when you reach your goal. People may tell you how great you look, you may be able to see it in photos, or when you try on a new outfit in the dressing room of the store, but on a daily basis, you may not know you've lost much weight. This is actually normal. Our self image gets set somewhere along the way and it is very difficult to change it.

It is somewhat like seeing your own aging. People will often say they woke up one day and were old. Of course that's not how it happens but it is a bit like watching grass grow. Since you are with yourself constantly, the small changes are hard to notice. We can't tell when we are gaining and sometimes the reverse is also true.

There may also be some disappointment if you were not able to get down to your original goal, or maintain it. That is OK and normal. Your goal may have been 130 lbs. but you may only be able to get to 140 lbs. It is the difference of 100 calories a day but it may just be too much for you to do without. If you let that be OK for now, and you get the hang of maintaining 140 lbs., you can always work on bringing it down in the future. The danger here is that people will be very all or nothing, black or white, and feel like a failure because they didn't get to goal and/or can't maintain it. This feeling has sent some back to their top weight and higher. Don't let that happen to you.

Take Credit for Your Successes

I read once that people with weight problems have two personality traits in common. Those are: they don't take credit for their successes and they put other people's needs ahead of their own. When it comes to weight loss, we want to take credit for the success. We want to relish it, enjoy it fully and know that it was and is being earned on a daily basis. You know how many people out there would love to lose weight and yet they don't do the work. If you have done the work and succeeded at losing weight, congratulate yourself. Take credit for it because it is hard work and it didn't just happen to you.

This personality trait should be worked on in other areas as well. We have to learn how to take credit for our successes across the board as a way to build our self-esteem. When you have been heavy, you can feel less than. This feeling of less than can carry into all areas of your life. That needs to turn around so you can feel just as good as. The most important way to do this is to take credit where credit is due. Weight loss isn't a gift that was given to you. You earned it and you deserve it.

If you are someone who has always put other people's needs ahead of your own, and that has contributed to your weight problems, it is time to start putting yourself on your list of priorities. This can feel selfish at first, but is worth doing and getting used to. It took a certain amount of self focus to lose the weight and it will take that same self focus and self care to maintain it. Don't forget that and let your hard work get lost in the sea of other people's demands and needs. Your needs matter too and deserve to be met. You will be a better parent, spouse, friend, family and community member if you are happy and healthy.

But All My Problems Aren't Solved and I'm Thin

If you were someone who used to dream about what it would be like when you got thin, you may be a bit disappointed in the reality of it. Some of my clients will start out thinking, "When I get thin, I will find love, get married, be beautiful/handsome, get hit on all the time, get good jobs, be treated better, etc… All my problems will be solved."

While some of these things may actually happen, some of them may not as well. Losing weight is very rewarding, but it doesn't fix everything in your life. In fact, it may cause some new problems. You may not be used to the extra attention, or be angry that people are nicer to you now that you are thin. That's OK and should be expected.

When we get thinner, so many things can change. What we wear, how we sit, walk, run, relate to others and how others relate to us. Friendships, marriages and family relationships can all change, either for the better or worse. When we change, the people around us have to change as well if they want to keep us in their lives. People, in general, don't like change. Your friends, family and coworkers have always known you as the heavy one. They are comfortable with you in that role. When you step out of the comfort zone, they have to adapt and they don't want to. They didn't change, after all, so why are you inconveniencing them by making them change to adapt to the new you. This is not very conscious, in general, but tends to go on just the same.

We want everyone to be happy and joyous about our weight loss. Some people in your life may be genuinely happy for you but those who feel threatened may not feel that way.

Knowing this can help you ride it out. Those who really love you will adjust in time. We need to allow ourselves time to change and we need to allow those around us time to adjust as well. Just make sure you don't let others cause you to start gaining weight back just to make them more comfortable. Just as the first two years of weight maintenance are the most difficult for the maintainer, they are also the most difficult for those around us who are adjusting as well. Once you get through the first two years of maintaining your weight loss, the people closest to you will also have gotten used to the new you and should have adjusted to the change by then.

This Weight Work Has Ruined My Ability to Binge

I'm sorry to tell you this, but losing weight and keeping it off will ruin your ability to binge with abandon. Once you are committed to keeping records, have lost weight, are aware of the amounts of calories and the portion sizes of the foods you are consuming, you can no longer fall asleep at the wheel and binge like you used to.

Leslie lost over 100 pounds and was concerned that she might gain it back someday. She said, "What happens if I unplug and forget everything?" I told her that she could never completely unplug once she had learned how to do this work. That even if she did unplug, the cord would be dangling and would get in her way. That annoying cord would never allow her to go all the way back to where she had been.

Leslie did find that she would occasionally overeat, and have high calorie days, but after 3 years of maintaining her 100 pound loss, she would return to her new behaviors quickly and catch herself before she gained much weight back. Her new life, and her health, meant too much to her to allow her to go back to her old ways.

120 Days

120 days are the number of days each year that include weekends, holidays and vacations. That is 1/3 of the year. If you allow yourself to go off track on all those days, you will only get 2/3 of your goal. Additionally, if you go off that often, you are not likely to go right back on. Being good all week and then going wild on the weekend is never a good strategy.

If you know you are going out with friends and want to enjoy yourself, you can bank calories for that. You can either have some low calorie days leading up to it and/or have a very low calorie day prior to the party so you have some calories to spend.

Keep in mind that there is no such thing as a weight loss credit card. If you overspend, or take in more calories than you burn, your body will store that as fat. It doesn't put it on an account that you can pay off over time. It puts it on as fat that you can lose over time, but you will have to carry it around until you are able to get rid of it.

Don't Go On Food Vacations

Lonny lost over 80 pounds and learned to maintain that weight during the year until summer came along. Lonny had a vacation home by a lake in Idaho and would go there every summer and spend 6 weeks enjoying the lake, his home and his boat. His entire family looked forward to that trip, each summer and so did Lonny. The trouble was, Lonny used those 6 weeks not just as a vacation from his regular life, but also as a food vacation. While he was there he would put aside all his weight loss behaviors and allow himself to eat with abandon. He would stop keeping records, paying attention to the calories and would indulge in his favorite coconut cream pie that was only available at this little diner near his Idaho home. Lonny looked as forward to the food as he did the rest of the vacation experience.

Every year he would come back about 13 pounds heavier than he had been when he left. It would take him a couple of months to work his weight back down and he would maintain it until he went back to Idaho. The problem with this behavior is that it set Lonny up into a type of binge/purge mentality. Eat like crazy for 6 weeks and then diet like crazy to get the weight back down. This is dangerous because there is no guarantee that you will be able to get it back down. In fact, Lonny found it was getting increasingly difficult to lose the weight when he got back from his trip. As he was getting older and busier in a new career, the weight loss was slowing down and getting harder.

Now, after maintaining most of his weight loss for 13 years, Lonny has gotten his vacation weight gain down to 7 pounds. That is about half of what it used to be. He is now able to get back down to his pre-Idaho weight relatively quickly.

I don't advocate going on food vacations at all. If you can learn to live at the weight you want to be, you can incorporate any food into your calorie budget, even coconut cream pie. You can travel the world, enjoy yourself without over-indulging and feel good when you get back from your trip. Coming back from a thrilling vacation can be depressing enough. It is even more depressing if you are coming home to a large weight gain.

The Journey Continues

There is no such thing as getting there and then going back to your old ways. Your old ways will take you back to your top weight. If more people understood that, I think we'd see less yo-yo dieting and more weight maintenance.

You never need to go on another diet if you are willing to keep track of your calories and your weight. You will have learned the key to long term weight control and will be free to enjoy your life in a healthy body. Will you sometimes miss your old food choices? Of course. Will you miss that big, uncomfortable body you had to live in 24/7? Of course not.

Congratulations on getting this far. Stay on the path, keep up the great work, and be well!

Chapter 7 Exercises:

1. Make sure you kept at least one item of clothing that you wore at your top weight. Whenever you get discouraged and/or complacent, put it on.

2. Remember that the work it took to get thin, is the same work you have to do to stay thin. Repeat the mantra, "It's worth it!"

3. Be grateful for your success. Very few have been able to accomplish this and maintain it.

4. Keep up the great work!

References

Kessler, David A. *The End of Overeating: Taking Control of the Insatiable American Appetite*. Emmaus, PA: Rodale, 2009. Print.

Roth, Geneen. *When Food Is Love: Exploring the Relationship between Eating and Intimacy*. New York, N.Y., U.S.A.: Dutton, 1991. Print.

Sheppard, Kay. *Food Addiction: Healing Day by Day : Daily Affirmations*. Deerfield Beach, FL: Health Communications, 2003. Print.

McKenna, Paul. *I Can Make You Thin: the Revolutionary System Used by More than 3 Million People*. New York: Sterling, 2009. Print.

Hirschmann, Jane R., and Carol H. Munter. *Overcoming Overeating*. Philadelphia, PA: Da Capo/Lifelong, 2008. Print.

Johnson, Richard J., and Timothy Gower. *The Sugar Fix: the High-fructose Fallout That Is Making You Fat and Sick*.

Emmaus, PA: Rodale, 2008. Print.

Brownell, Kelly D., and Katherine Battle. Horgen. *Food Fight: the inside Story of the Food Industry, America's Obesity Crisis, and What We Can Do about It*. Chicago: Contemporary, 2004. Print.

Heber, David, and Susan Bowerman. *What Color Is Your Diet?: the 7 Colors of Health*. New York, NY: Regan, 2001. Print.

Kübler-Ross, Elisabeth. *On Death and Dying.* [New York]: Macmillan, 1969. Print.

Klem ML, Wing RR, McGuire MT, Seagle HM & Hill JO (1997). A descriptive study of individuals successful at long-term maintenance of substantial weight loss.*American Journal of Clinical Nutrition*, 66, 239-246.

Shick SM, Wing RR, Klem ML, McGuire MT, Hill JO & Seagle HM (1998). Persons successful at long-term weight loss and maintenance continue to consume a low calorie, low fat diet. *Journal of the American Dietetic Association*, 98, 408-413.

Wyatt HR, Grunwald GK, Seagle HM, Klem ML, McGuire MT, Wing RR & Hill JO. (1999). Resting energy expenditure in reduced-obese subjects in the National Weight Control Registry. *American Journal of Clinical Nutrition*, 69, 1189-1193.

McGuire MT, Wing RR, Klem ML, Lang W & Hill JO. (1999). What predicts weight regain among a group of successful weight losers? *Journal of Consulting & Clinical Psychology*, 67, 177-185.

Phelan S, Wing RR, Hill JO, Dibello J. (2003). Recovery from relapse among successful weight maintainers. *American Journal of Clinical Nutrition*, 78, 1079- 1084.

Butryn ML, Phelan S, Hill JO, Wing RR. (2007). Consistent Self-monitoring of Weight: A Key Component of Successful Weight Loss Maintenance. *Obesity*, 15, 3091-3096.

Acknowledgements

THIS BOOK WOULD NOT EXIST without the help of so many fabulous people. First I'd like to thank each and every one of you who took the time to take the survey. Your heartfelt answers and stories appear in the pages of the book and inform this work in many important ways.

I'd also like to thank Gayle Pikna, my tireless editor for helping me refine the manuscript and for making the book better!

My fantastic agent, Laurie Harper, you're the best. Laurie believed in this book from the start. Thank you!

To Frances Ehrmann for her valuable input into the book in its early stages.

To all of my clients and support group members, thank you for teaching me so much. Your stories are in the book and your successes inspire me everyday.

Thank you to my Huffington Post © readers for your comments over the last few years. Your input is in the book and is greatly appreciated!

And to my husband George for believing in me and in this book and for pushing me to get it done and out there.

To my son, Jack, for staying quiet enough for me to work. Thank you!

CPSIA information can be obtained
at www.ICGtesting.com
Printed in the USA
BVHW01s1625040118
504320BV00002B/125/P

9 781936 780754